Bitcoin Breakthrough

Bitcoin Decoded: A Comprehensive Overview of the Pioneering Cryptocurrency

Max Harper

Table of Contents

INTRODUCTION

Welcome to "Bitcoin Breakthrough: Bitcoin Decoded- A Comprehensive Overview of the Pioneering Cryptocurrency." We go on an insightful journey to understand the nuances of Bitcoin, the revolutionary digital currency that has completely changed the way we think about money, finance, and technology, in this book.

The world was captivated by the revolutionary blockchain technology of Bitcoin, the first decentralized cryptocurrency that was founded in 2009 by the mysterious persona known only as Satoshi Nakamoto. Since its launch, Bitcoin has experienced unheard-of growth that has sparked heated discussions and piqued the curiosity of investors, technologists, and financial enthusiasts alike.

We go deeply into the principles of Bitcoin in this book, explaining the intricacies of its underlying technology and examining its significant effects on international banking, economics, and society. This book aims to provide you a thorough knowledge of Bitcoin's essence, function, and potential—regardless of your experience with cryptocurrencies.

We will examine the blockchain technology concepts underpinning the security and decentralization of Bitcoin in the following chapters. We will explore the fascinating mechanism that maintains the integrity and scarcity of Bitcoin—the mining process. We will also explore the different aspects of the Bitcoin network, including wallets, fees, and transactions, and we will figure out the mechanisms that allow it to operate as a peer-to-peer digital payment system.

Through this book, we will look at the financial and economic effects of Bitcoin's supply limitation and its potential as an asset for future investments and as a store of value. In addition, we will examine the shifting regulatory environment surrounding Bitcoin and discuss the issues and disputes related to its usage.

Moreover, this book will consider how Bitcoin might promote financial inclusion by filling the gap for unbanked and underprivileged people across the globe. We'll examine case studies of how Bitcoin has been adopted in underdeveloped countries and the opportunities it offers for a more diverse global economy.

Notwithstanding the popularity and success of Bitcoin, we will also analyze its drawbacks, including energy consumption and scalability problems, and the efforts being made to solve them. We'll be thinking about how cryptocurrencies are changing and what the future holds for Bitcoin in the quickly changing financial landscape as we explore.

We welcome you to immerse yourself in the Bitcoin world as we embark on this discovery journey. From its beginnings to its revolutionary possibilities, this book seeks to shed light on the core of this trailblazing cryptocurrency, giving you a thorough and perceptive rundown.

Together, we will unravel the mysteries and seize the opportunities presented by Bitcoin, the decentralized revolution that is fundamentally altering our understanding of money and the direction of finance. Join us on this insightful journey.

CHAPTER I

Understanding Bitcoin

What is Bitcoin?

Bitcoin: a groundbreaking and enigmatic phenomenon that has revolutionized the financial landscape and captured the world's imagination since its inception in 2009. Created by the pseudonymous figure Satoshi Nakamoto, Bitcoin is the first decentralized cryptocurrency, built upon a revolutionary technology called blockchain. In this section, we will delve into the fundamental aspects of Bitcoin, its underlying principles, the technology that powers it, and its significance in the modern world.

Bitcoin emerged amidst the backdrop of the global financial crisis of 2008, a period marked by faltering trust in traditional financial institutions and centralized governance. Nakamoto's whitepaper, titled "Bitcoin: A Peer-to-Peer Electronic Cash System," introduced the concept of a digital currency that operates outside the control of any central authority. At its core, the vision was to create a borderless, censorship-resistant, and transparent form of money that empowers individuals with financial autonomy. Bitcoin's creation aimed to address the flaws of the existing financial system, allowing people to transact directly with each other, irrespective of geographical boundaries or intermediaries.

At the heart of Bitcoin lies its groundbreaking technology called blockchain. Blockchain is a ledger that is distributed that tracks every Bitcoin transaction across a node—a network of computers. Each block on the chain contains a batch of transactions, and once a block is added, it becomes a permanent part of the blockchain. Every transaction on the blockchain is guaranteed to be transparent, safe, and impenetrable due to its decentralized and immutable nature. This ground-breaking technology underpins the Bitcoin monetary system and has broad ramifications across a range of sectors, including voting systems, healthcare, and supply chain management.

Bitcoin's security and consensus are maintained through a process known as mining. Mining involves validating and adding new transactions to the blockchain while creating new bitcoins in the process. Miners compete to solve complicated mathematical puzzles, and the first to solve them is to add the following block to the blockchain. This proof-of-work consensus mechanism ensures that no single entity can control the network and safeguards against potential attacks. However, the mining process also consumes significant computational power and electricity, leading to ongoing discussions about its environmental impact.

One of Bitcoin's most unique features is its fixed supply. The overall number of bitcoins that will ever exist is capped at 21 million, a predetermined limit embedded in the protocol. This scarcity is in stark contrast to fiat currencies that can be printed endlessly by central banks. As more people adopt Bitcoin and the mining process continues, the rate at which new bitcoins are created decreases through periodic halving events. This deflationary monetary policy is designed to combat inflation and preserve the value of Bitcoin over time, making it a potential hedge against traditional currency devaluation.

Bitcoin transactions are facilitated through digital wallets, which store the public and private keys necessary for sending and receiving bitcoins. Public keys function as addresses, allowing users to receive funds, while private keys are utilized to sign transactions and access the bitcoins stored in the wallet. Proper key management is crucial as losing a private key could result in irreversible loss of funds. Wallets come in various forms, including software, hardware, and paper wallets, each with its own advantages and security considerations.

Bitcoin transactions are conducted directly between users, and each transaction is broadcast to the network. Miners select transactions from the pool, verify their validity, and include them in a new block to add to the blockchain. Once a transaction is included in a block, it receives its first confirmation, and with each subsequent block, the number of confirmations increases. More confirmations enhance the security and finality of a transaction, making it increasingly difficult to reverse.

Bitcoin's decentralization and cryptographic security provide several advantages, such as fast and low-cost cross-border transactions, financial inclusion for the unbanked, and protection against inflation and capital controls. Additionally, Bitcoin offers a level of privacy, as transactions do not require personal information. However, Bitcoin also faces challenges, including its price volatility, scalability issues, regulatory uncertainties, and concerns about its environmental impact due to energy-intensive mining operations.

As Bitcoin gained popularity, governments and financial regulators worldwide began grappling with its implications and sought ways to regulate its use. The regulatory approach varies across countries, with some embracing Bitcoin as a legitimate asset class, while others remain cautious or outright ban its use. Balancing innovation, consumer protection, and financial stability remains a complex and ongoing endeavor for policymakers.

Bitcoin's future is subject to continuous evolution and adaptation. Technical improvements like the Lightning Network address scalability and transaction speed concerns, making Bitcoin more viable for day-to-day transactions. Institutional adoption, increased regulatory clarity, and growing public interest could further solidify Bitcoin's position in the global financial landscape. However, challenges, such as governance decisions and potential competition from other cryptocurrencies, continue to shape the future trajectory of Bitcoin.

Brief history of Bitcoin's creation

The inception of Bitcoin marked the beginning of a new era in finance and technology, revolutionizing the way we perceive money and transactions. Created in 2009 by an anonymous entity, Satoshi Nakamoto, Bitcoin emerged as the world's first decentralized cryptocurrency. In this section, we will embark on a journey through time, exploring the key milestones and events that shaped the creation and early days of Bitcoin, from its conceptualization to its widespread recognition as a groundbreaking innovation.

The origins of Bitcoin trace back to a whitepaper with a title of "Bitcoin: A Peer-to-Peer Electronic Cash System," published in October 2008. In this seminal paper, Nakamoto presented a vision of a digital currency that would enable direct transactions between parties without intermediaries or centralized control. The whitepaper outlined the fundamental principles of Bitcoin, including its use of blockchain technology, decentralized consensus mechanism, and the fixed supply of 21 million coins.

On January 3, 2009, the first-ever Bitcoin block, known as the "genesis block," was mined by Nakamoto. This momentous event marked the official launch of the Bitcoin network, and it contained a message referencing a headline from The Times newspaper that day: "Chancellor on brink of second bailout for banks." This embedded message underscored Nakamoto's motivation for creating Bitcoin - to offer an alternative financial system that operates independently from traditional banking institutions and their potential failures.

In the early days of Bitcoin, Nakamoto worked closely with other early adopters and developers to refine the cryptocurrency's code and establish a community around it. The initial version of the Bitcoin software was released as open-source, allowing anyone to review and contribute to its development. This collaborative approach laid the foundation for Bitcoin's decentralized governance, a core principle that continues to shape its evolution.

As Bitcoin gained traction, it started to attract a small but passionate community of users, developers, and enthusiasts. In 2010, Bitcoin made headlines when a developer named Laszlo Hanyecz conducted the first real-world transaction using the cryptocurrency. He famously purchased two pizzas for 10,000 bitcoins, which, at the time, held a nominal value of a few dollars. This transaction demonstrated the potential of Bitcoin as a medium of exchange, albeit one that was still in its nascent stages.

Bitcoin faced praise and skepticism from various quarters in the following years. While some lauded its potential to disrupt the financial status quo and foster financial inclusion, others expressed concerns about its use in illicit activities and the lack of regulatory oversight. These discussions led to ongoing debates about the advantages and challenges of decentralized cryptocurrencies and their potential impact on the global economy.

One of the significant milestones in Bitcoin's history was the introduction of Mt. Gox, a Tokyo-based Bitcoin exchange, in 2010. Mt. Gox played a crucial role in facilitating Bitcoin's early adoption, providing a platform for users to purchase and sell bitcoins with fiat currencies. However, in 2014, Mt. Gox experienced a catastrophic security breach, leading to the loss of hundreds of thousands of bitcoins and the eventual closure of the exchange. The incident highlighted the importance of security and user protection in the cryptocurrency ecosystem.

Over the years, Bitcoin underwent numerous technical advancements and improvements. In 2012, the first Bitcoin halving occurred, reducing the block reward for miners from 50 to 25 bitcoins. This halving event, designed to appear approximately every four years, served to limit the rate of new coin issuance, contributing to Bitcoin's deflationary monetary policy.

Bitcoin's price volatility also garnered significant attention during this period. The cryptocurrency experienced several price bubbles and subsequent corrections, with its value reaching all-time highs, followed by periods of substantial decline. These price fluctuations fueled debates about Bitcoin's suitability as a stable store of value and its potential for mainstream adoption.

In 2017, Bitcoin's price skyrocketed to unprecedented levels, capturing global media attention and sparking a surge in public interest and investment. The meteoric rise in value also led to congestion on the Bitcoin network, resulting in higher transaction fees and longer processing times. This scaling challenge prompted discussions and proposals for solutions to improve Bitcoin's transaction throughput.

Bitcoin's increasing popularity also brought it under the scrutiny of governments and regulatory bodies worldwide. Various countries grappled with classifying and regulating cryptocurrency, resulting in a patchwork of approaches, ranging from embracing its potential to imposing restrictions on its use.

Despite the challenges and fluctuations, Bitcoin grew as a financial asset and an influential force in the broader blockchain and cryptocurrency ecosystem. Several other cryptocurrencies, commonly called altcoins, were launched, inspired by Bitcoin's success and aiming to address different use cases and technological innovations.

As the technology and infrastructure supporting Bitcoin matured, more businesses and institutions began to explore its potential applications. Major companies started accepting Bitcoin as a form of payment, and financial institutions delved into research and development related to blockchain technology.

Importance and impact of Bitcoin in the financial world

Bitcoin, the pioneering cryptocurrency introduced in 2009 by an anonymous entity known as Satoshi Nakamoto, has evolved from an obscure digital experiment to a transformative force in the global financial landscape. Its decentralized nature and groundbreaking blockchain technology have catalyzed a paradigm shift, challenging traditional financial systems and reshaping how we perceive money, transactions, and value. In this section, we explore the importance and multifaceted impact of Bitcoin in the financial world, encompassing its role as a store of value, medium of exchange, investment asset, and harbinger of financial inclusion.

Bitcoin's emergence as a store of value has been one of its most significant contributions to the financial world. Traditionally, fiat currencies and assets like gold served as stores of value, but they were susceptible to inflation and fluctuations driven by central bank policies and geopolitical events. With its fixed supply and deflationary nature, Bitcoin offers an alternative form of wealth preservation. Its capped total supply of 21 million coins creates scarcity and hedges against traditional currency devaluation. As geopolitical uncertainties loom and traditional markets exhibit volatility, investors increasingly turn to Bitcoin as a safe-haven asset, a digital "digital gold" that can potentially protect their wealth from economic uncertainties and market turbulence.

Beyond its role as a store of value, Bitcoin has demonstrated its potential as a medium of exchange, enabling fast, secure, and borderless transactions. Traditional financial systems often entail lengthy and costly cross-border transactions, especially in regions with limited banking infrastructure. Bitcoin's decentralized nature allows users to transact directly with each other, bypassing intermediaries and reducing transaction fees. This aspect has significant implications for remittances and cross-border trade, as Bitcoin can facilitate quicker and cheaper funds transfers across borders, particularly in regions where traditional financial services are less accessible.

Moreover, Bitcoin's attributes as a medium of exchange extend to its utility in facilitating micropayments and online transactions. Its divisibility into smaller units, known as satoshis, enables the transfer of minute amounts, making it suitable for use in microtransactions and internet-based commerce. This potential has garnered interest from content creators, allowing them to receive direct support from their audiences without relying on payment processors that often charge high fees.

The growth of Bitcoin as an investment asset has captured the attention of institutional and retail investors alike. As the first cryptocurrency to gain widespread recognition, Bitcoin has seen major price appreciation over the years, attracting speculative interest from investors seeking to capitalize on its potential for high returns. Additionally, the growing interest in Bitcoin as a portfolio diversifier has further contributed to its importance in the financial world. Investors see Bitcoin as an asset that exhibits a low correlation with conventional financial markets, which can offer benefits in reducing overall portfolio risk.

However, Bitcoin's emergence as an investment asset has also brought scrutiny and regulatory challenges. Governments and financial regulators worldwide have grappled with how to classify and regulate cryptocurrencies. The evolving regulatory landscape has implications for investor protection, taxation, and market integrity. As the cryptocurrency market grows, policymakers face the delicate task of balancing fostering innovation and safeguarding consumer interests.

Bitcoin's impact on the financial world extends beyond its usage as a store of value, medium of exchange, and investment asset. Cryptocurrency has acted as a catalyst for financial inclusion, offering a potential solution for the billions of unbanked and underbanked individuals worldwide. In many developing countries, access to traditional financial services is limited, leaving large portions of the population excluded from the formal banking system. Bitcoin's decentralized nature allows anyone with internet access to participate in the network and access financial services, opening new avenues for economic empowerment.

Additionally, Bitcoin's potential for financial inclusion goes beyond geographic boundaries. In regions facing economic instability, currency devaluation, and capital controls, citizens have sought refuge in cryptocurrencies like Bitcoin to protect their wealth and gain access to a global financial network that transcends national borders. By providing a financial lifeline to the unbanked and those grappling with economic hardships, Bitcoin is a powerful tool for promoting financial autonomy and economic resilience.

As Bitcoin's importance and impact have grown, so has its surrounding ecosystem. An entire industry has emerged, spanning exchanges, wallets, payment processors, mining operations, and blockchain-based applications. This burgeoning industry has provided employment opportunities and spurred innovation in financial technology, encouraging new entrepreneurs and developers to create innovative solutions that leverage blockchain technology.

Nevertheless, Bitcoin's rapid ascent has not been without challenges and criticism. Price volatility, scalability concerns, and energy-intensive mining have been subjects of debate and ongoing improvements. The quest for scalability and transaction throughput has led to exploring second-layer solutions like the Lightning Network, which aims to facilitate faster and more cost-effective transactions.

CHAPTER II

Understanding Blockchain Technology

Introduction to blockchain

Blockchain technology has rapidly emerged as a transformative force across various industries, reshaping how we conduct transactions, secure data, and manage digital assets. A blockchain is fundamentally a distributed ledger that securely, transparently, and permanently records transactions. This section delves into the fundamental concepts of blockchain, its underlying principles, and its potential applications.

An unidentified person going by the name of Satoshi Nakamoto published a whitepaper in 2008, which is when the blockchain concept first emerged. Nakamoto's whitepaper introduced Bitcoin, the world's first cryptocurrency, serving as the foundational blockchain technology use case. Blockchain, in essence, is a decentralized digital ledger consisting of a block chain, each containing a list of transactions. These blocks are linked in chronological order, forming a continuous and unchangeable data chain.

One of the fundamental features of blockchain is its decentralization. Unlike traditional centralized systems, where a single entity controls data and transactions, blockchain operates on a peer-to-peer network. This means no single entity, such as a bank or government, has sole authority over the blockchain. Instead, transactions are verified by a network of participants (nodes) through a consensus mechanism, like Proof of Work (or PoW) or Proof of Stake (or PoS). This decentralization enhances security, transparency, and trust in the system, as there is no central point of failure.

Immutability is another crucial aspect of blockchain. Once data is recorded in a block, it becomes challenging, if not impossible, to alter or delete. This is accomplished by the use of cryptographic hashing, in which every block has a distinct cryptographic hash of the block before it. Any change to the data in a block would require the consensus of most network participants, making fraudulent activities highly improbable.

Security is paramount in the digital age, and blockchain offers a robust solution. Cryptography plays a central role in securing blockchain transactions. Public and private keys are used to authenticate users and authorize transactions. This makes sure that the only individual who can access and manage their assets on the blockchain is the owner of a private key. Furthermore, because blockchain is decentralized and lacks a central point that could be hacked, there is a lower chance of cyberattacks and data breaches.

Beyond just cryptocurrencies, blockchain technology has the power to completely transform a number of industries. For instance, smart contracts serve as self-executing agreements that have the conditions of the contract directly encoded into the code. These contracts reduce the need for middlemen and the likelihood of disputes by automatically executing when predetermined conditions are met. To improve efficiency and transparency, blockchain is being investigated by a number of industries, including finance, real estate, healthcare, as well as supply chain management.

In conclusion, blockchain is a groundbreaking technology with the potential to disrupt traditional systems and redefine how we conduct transactions and manage data. Its decentralized nature, immutability, and security features make it a powerful tool for various applications. As the technology evolves and gain wider acceptance, it is essential to understand its fundamental principles and explore its potential to drive innovation in diverse sectors of the economy. Blockchain is not merely a buzzword; it represents a fundamental shift in how we envision the future of digital transactions and data management.

How blockchain works

Blockchain technology has acquired significant attention for its potential to revolutionize various industries, but to understand its transformative power, it's essential to delve into how blockchain works at its core. At its heart, a blockchain is a distributed and decentralized ledger that records transactions securely and transparently. In this section we will navigate the inner workings of blockchain, from data structure to consensus mechanisms and its role in securing digital transactions.

A blockchain consists of a series of chained blocks, with each block having a list of transactions. These transactions can represent the transfer of assets, digital contracts, or any data that requires secure and transparent recording. The blocks are linked in chronological order, forming an unbroken data chain. This chain structure ensures that the history of transactions is preserved, creating a transparent and immutable record. One of the key features of blockchain is decentralization. Traditional systems rely on a central authority, such as a bank or government, to validate and record transactions.

In contrast, blockchain operates on a peer-to-peer network of computers, known as nodes. These nodes work together to validate and record transactions through a consensus mechanism. Common consensus mechanisms include PoW and PoS. In PoW, nodes compete to solve complicated mathematical puzzles, with the first to solve it adding a new block to the blockchain. PoS, on the other hand, relies on validators who are selected to create new blocks that depend on the amount of cryptocurrency they hold and are willing to "stake" as collateral.

Immutability is another fundamental aspect of blockchain. Once data is recorded in a block, it becomes challenging to alter or delete. This immutability is achieved through cryptographic hashing. Each block has a unique cryptographic hash of the previous block, creating a chain where altering the data in one block would require changing all subsequent blocks, which is computationally infeasible.

Security is paramount in the world of blockchain. Transactions on the blockchain are secured through public and private key cryptography. Users have a pair of cryptographic keys: a public key, which serves as their address on the blockchain, and a private key, which is kept secret and used to sign transactions. Only the holder of the private key can authorize transactions on their behalf. Furthermore, the decentralized nature of blockchain mitigates the risk of attacks. As opposed to centralized systems that have a single point of failure, a successful attack on a blockchain would require control of most network nodes, making it highly secure.

The transparency of the blockchain is another remarkable feature. Anyone can view the whole transaction history of a blockchain, as it's stored in a public ledger. This transparency enhances trust and accountability in the system, reducing the potential for fraud and corruption.

Blockchain technology has gone far beyond its initial application in cryptocurrencies like Bitcoin. Smart contracts, for instance, are self-executing contracts with code defining the terms of the agreement. These contracts automatically execute when predefined conditions are met, eliminating the requirement for intermediaries and reducing the risk of disputes.

In conclusion, blockchain is a groundbreaking technology operating on decentralization, immutability, security, and transparency principles. Its unique architecture and consensus mechanisms make it a powerful tool for many applications beyond cryptocurrencies. Understanding how blockchain works is essential for grasping its potential to transform industries by enhancing efficiency, security, and trust in digital transactions and data management. As this technology evolves, its impact on various sectors of the economy is likely to be profound.

Key features and benefits of blockchain technology

Blockchain technology has appeared as a revolutionary innovation with the potential to transform various industries. Its key features and benefits make it a compelling solution for many applications, beyond just cryptocurrencies. This section explores the fundamental features of blockchain and the significant advantages it offers to businesses and society as a whole.

One of the central features of blockchain is decentralization. Unlike traditional centralized systems, where a single entity controls data and transactions, blockchain operates on a distributed network of computers, known as nodes. These nodes work together to validate and record transactions through a consensus mechanism, like Proof of Work or Proof of Stake. Decentralization eliminates the need for intermediaries, reducing the risk of manipulation, censorship, and single points of failure. This feature fosters trust and transparency in the system.

Immutability is another critical aspect of blockchain. Once data is recorded in a block, it becomes challenging to alter or delete. This immutability is achieved through cryptographic hashing, where each block has a unique cryptographic hash of the previous block. Any change to the data in a block would require the consensus of most network participants, making fraudulent activities highly improbable. Immutability enhances the integrity of records, making blockchain a secure and dependable platform for data storage and transactions.

Security is paramount in the digital age, and blockchain technology offers robust security features. Transactions on the blockchain are secured through public and private key cryptography. Users have a pair of cryptographic keys: a public key, which serves as their address on the blockchain, and a private key, which is kept secret and used to sign transactions. Only the holder of the private key can authorize transactions on their behalf. Additionally, the decentralized nature of blockchain reduces the risk of cyberattacks and data breaches, as there is no central point vulnerable to hacking.

One of the defining characteristic of blockchain technology is transparency. Since a blockchain's transaction history is kept on a public ledger, anybody may see it. This transparency enhances trust and accountability in the system, reducing the potential for fraud and corruption. It also allows for improved auditing and traceability, making blockchain suitable for various industries, including supply chain management, where tracking the origin and journey of products is critical.

Another significant benefit of blockchain is its efficiency. Traditional financial systems can involve multiple intermediaries and complex processes that lead to delays and higher costs. Blockchain streamlines these processes by enabling peer-to-peer transactions and automated smart contracts. Smart contracts act as self-executing agreements that have been encoded directly into the code. When certain circumstances are met, they automatically take action, removing the need for middlemen and lowering the possibility of disagreements. This effectiveness can result in lower costs and quicker transaction times for a variety of businesses.

Blockchain technology has the ability to innovate and upend several industries, such as supply chain management, healthcare, and finance. Its key features of decentralization, immutability, security, and transparency, along with the benefits of efficiency and reduced costs, make it a powerful tool for businesses seeking to enhance their operations and build customer trust. As blockchain evolves and gain wider adoption, its influence on the global economy and society will likely be profound, reshaping how we transact, manage data, and interact in the digital world.

CHAPTER III

Bitcoin Mining and Consensus Mechanism

Mining process and its role in securing the network

Blockchain technology has received widespread recognition for its decentralized, transparent, and secure nature. At the core of this innovative technology lies the mining process, a fundamental mechanism responsible for adding new blocks to the blockchain and guaranteeing the security as well as integrity of the entire network. Mining plays a crucial role in achieving consensus among nodes, preventing double-spending, and incentivizing participants to contribute their computational power to the network. This section delves into the intricacies of the mining process, exploring its role in securing the network, the challenges it faces, and the potential impact on the blockchain ecosystem.

The mining process is the backbone of the Proof of Work (PoW) consensus mechanism, which serves as the foundation for many well-known cryptocurrencies like Bitcoin. It involves validating and bundling new transactions into blocks, which are then added to the blockchain. To accomplish this, miners must solve complex mathematical puzzles based on the data in the new transactions. The first miner to find the solution for the puzzle is able to add the new block to the chain and will gain a reward in the form of cryptocurrency. This competitive process incentivizes miners to contribute their computational power to the network, ensuring the blockchain remains secure and resilient.

Mining is crucial in securing the blockchain network. PoW requires miners to perform computationally intensive calculations to find a specific number, known as the "nonce," that, when combined with the block's data, results in a hash with a certain number of leading zeros. This process is known as "hashing," and it ensures that finding the correct nonce is a trial-and-error process, as there is no shortcut or deterministic method to solve the puzzle. The complexity of the mining process makes it challenging for malicious actors to create fraudulent blocks and attempt double-spending, as it would require an immense amount of computational power and time to rewrite the blockchain's history.

Incentives play a significant role in the mining process. Mining is resource-intensive, and miners incur electricity, hardware, and maintenance costs. To motivate miners to participate in the process and secure the network, they are rewarded with newly minted cryptocurrency and transaction fees paid by users. This reward system ensures that miners are motivated to confirm transactions as well as add new blocks to the chain, allowing them to earn a return on their investment in hardware and computational power. The block reward also serves as an inflation control mechanism, controlling the supply of new cryptocurrency in circulation.

The mining process is vital for achieving consensus among all nodes in the blockchain network. Once a miner successfully solves the puzzle and adds a new block to the chain, other network nodes verify the block's validity and its transactions. If most nodes agree that the new block is valid, it becomes part of the blockchain, and the transaction is confirmed. This consensus mechanism ensures that all participants in the network have an up-to-date and consistent copy of the blockchain, promoting trust and preventing double-spending.

Challenges exist within the mining process. As the popularity of blockchain networks increases, more miners join the competition, making it harder to solve the mathematical puzzles. To maintain a consistent block generation time, the difficulty of the puzzles is adjusted based on the overall network's computational power. However, increasing difficulty levels can lead to centralization, as large mining operations with substantial computational power become more likely to solve the puzzles and receive the block rewards. Smaller miners may find competing and receiving rewards increasingly challenging in such a competitive environment.

Another challenge associated with the mining process is its energy consumption. The PoW consensus mechanism, while secure and proven, is notorious for its high energy usage. The mining process involves numerous miners competing to solve puzzles, leading to significant electricity consumption and carbon emissions. Critics argue that the energy-intensive nature of PoW is unsustainable and contributes to environmental concerns, primarily when powered by fossil fuels. As a response, some blockchain networks are exploring alternative consensus mechanisms, such as PoS, which require less computational power and offer potential energy efficiency gains.

The rise of mining pools has become a significant development within the mining ecosystem. As the mining difficulty increases, individual miners face a diminishing chance of successfully mining a block and earning the reward. To increase their chances, miners often join mining pools, where multiple participants combine their computational power to solve puzzles and share the rewards collectively. Mining pools have become prevalent, especially in large-scale mining operations. They allow smaller miners to have a more consistent income and reduce the reward variance. However, the rise of mining pools also raises concerns about centralization, as a few large pools can potentially control most of the network's mining power, leading to concentration and possible manipulation of the network.

The potential impact of the mining process on the blockchain ecosystem is a subject of ongoing debate and research. While PoW has proven to be a robust and secure consensus mechanism, concerns about its energy consumption and centralization have prompted the exploration of alternative approaches. PoS, for instance, relies on validators who "stake" their cryptocurrency as collateral to validate transactions and add new blocks to the chain. Validators are selected depending on the number of coins they are willing to "stake" and how long they have held those coins. PoS offers potential energy savings and may address some of the centralization concerns associated with PoW.

Proof of Work vs. Proof of Stake

Blockchain technology has revolutionized various industries, introducing innovative solutions and reshaping traditional systems. At the core of blockchain networks are consensus mechanisms, which determine how transactions are validated and added to the blockchain. Two prominent consensus mechanisms are Proof of Work (PoW) and Proof of Stake (PoS). PoW, popularized by Bitcoin, was the first consensus mechanism, while PoS has gained traction due to its potential for energy efficiency and reduced centralization. This section delves into a comprehensive comparative analysis of PoW and PoS, exploring their underlying principles, advantages, disadvantages, and potential impact on the future of blockchain networks.

The initial consensus method, known as Proof of Work, was first presented by Satoshi Nakamoto in the 2008 Bitcoin whitepaper. Miners compete in PoW by using the data from new transactions to solve challenging mathematical puzzles. The chance to add an additional block to the blockchain and get paid in cryptocurrency is given to the first miner to figure out the puzzle. The difficulty of the puzzles is adjusted regularly to maintain a consistent block generation time. PoW ensures security by making the process resource-intensive, requiring miners to invest computational power and energy to participate in the network. The longer the blockchain becomes, the more secure it becomes, as altering any block would require re-mining all subsequent blocks, which is practically infeasible.

PoW has several advantages that contribute to its widespread adoption. Firstly, it has a proven track record and has demonstrated its security and resilience in the Bitcoin network for over a decade. The robustness of PoW stems from its resource-intensive nature, making it difficult for malicious actors to control most of the network's computational power and manipulate the blockchain. Secondly, PoW encourages decentralization, as miners worldwide can participate in the mining process, ensuring a diverse and distributed network. Thirdly, PoW offers a clear and straightforward method for determining the validity of transactions and achieving consensus among nodes.

Despite its successes, PoW has its disadvantages. The primary concern is its significant energy consumption.

The mining process involves numerous miners competing to solve puzzles, leading to extensive electricity usage and carbon emissions. Critics argue that PoW's energy-intensive nature is unsustainable and contributes to environmental concerns, mainly when powered by fossil fuels. Additionally, the energy consumption associated with PoW can lead to high transaction fees, as miners need to cover their operational costs.

An alternate consensus method called proof of stake helps to allay some of the worries about proof of work (PoW). Depending on how many coins they are willing to "stake" as collateral, validators in proof of stake (PoS) are selected to build new blocks and approve transactions. Validators are incentivized to act honestly, as their staked coins can be "slashed" or forfeited if they validate fraudulent transactions. PoS aims to achieve consensus and secure the network without resource-intensive mining. PoS has gained popularity due to its potential for energy efficiency and reduced environmental impact compared to PoW.

PoS offers several advantages over PoW. Firstly, it consumes significantly less energy than PoW, as it does not rely on resource-intensive mining. This energy efficiency is an attractive feature for those concerned about the impact on the environment of blockchain networks. Secondly, PoS promotes decentralization by allowing anyone with coins to participate in the network as a validator. This inclusivity contrasts with PoW, where only miners with substantial computational power can effectively participate. Thirdly, PoS eliminates the need for specialized mining hardware, making it more accessible and cost-effective for participants.

While PoS offers many benefits, it also has its drawbacks. One primary concern is the "rich-get-richer" problem, where validators with a significant stake in the network have a higher chance of being selected to create new blocks and receive rewards. This concentration of wealth and power could lead to centralization and reduce blockchain networks' security and decentralization goals. Additionally, PoS introduces a potential attack vector, known as the "nothing-at-stake" problem, where validators may attempt to create multiple competing chains and double-spend without the same resource costs associated with PoW.

The debate between PoW and PoS revolves around their respective advantages and disadvantages. PoW's proven security and resilience make it an attractive option for networks with paramount properties, such as Bitcoin's focus on store-of-value and digital gold. However, concerns about its energy consumption have prompted some networks to explore alternatives like PoS. Ethereum, the world's second-largest cryptocurrency, is transitioning from PoW to PoS with Ethereum 2.0 to achieve higher scalability and energy efficiency.

In addition to PoW and PoS, various hybrid and alternative consensus mechanisms have emerged. One example is Delegated Proof of Stake (DPoS), where stakeholders vote for a limited number of delegates responsible for verifying transactions and adding new blocks. DPoS aims to improve scalability and reduce the potential for centralization by allowing stakeholders to have a more direct say in the network's governance.

Other approaches, such as Practical Byzantine Fault Tolerance (PBFT) and Proof of Authority (PoA), focus on achieving consensus in permissioned blockchain networks with known validators.

When choosing a consensus mechanism, blockchain developers must consider their network's specific goals and requirements. While PoW provides a proven and secure method for achieving consensus, it comes with high energy costs. PoS offers energy efficiency and inclusivity but raises concerns about centralization and nothing-at-stake attacks. The choice between PoW, PoS, or other consensus mechanisms depends on the network's use case, security requirements, decentralization goals, and environmental impact considerations.

Energy consumption and environmental concerns

Bitcoin, the pioneering cryptocurrency introduced by Satoshi Nakamoto in 2009, has garnered widespread attention and adoption over the years. At the heart of the Bitcoin network lies its consensus mechanism, Proof of Work (PoW), which ensures security and immutability through resource-intensive mining. However, the energy-intensive nature of Bitcoin mining has raised significant concerns about its environmental impact. This section delves into the energy consumption of Bitcoin mining, the environmental implications, and explores potential solutions and alternative consensus mechanisms to address these pressing challenges.

The process of creating new blocks and adding new transactions to the blockchain is known as Bitcoin mining. Utilizing the information in new transactions as a basis, miners compete to solve challenging mathematical puzzles called as Proof of Work. The first miner to figure out the puzzle gets to add an additional block to the blockchain and get paid in transaction fees and freshly created bitcoins. PoW ensures security by making the mining process computationally expensive, requiring miners to invest significant computational power and energy to participate in the network.

The amount of energy used in Bitcoin mining is currently being closely examined and discussed. The mining process involves numerous miners competing to solve the mathematical puzzles, which requires extensive computational power. Energy usage rises as a result of the puzzles' increasing difficulty as more miners join the network. According to estimates, Bitcoin's annual energy consumption has reached levels comparable to small countries, making it a significant contributor to global energy consumption.

The environmental implications of Bitcoin's energy consumption are a cause for concern. Most Bitcoin mining operations rely on fossil fuel-based energy sources, like the coal and natural gas, which contribute to climate change by emitting greenhouse gases. Mining operations are often concentrated in regions with access to cheap electricity, which may not necessarily come from renewable sources. As a result, Bitcoin mining's carbon footprint and environmental impact have raised questions about the sustainability of the network in the long term.

Critics argue that the energy-intensive nature of Bitcoin mining contradicts the growing global efforts to transition to sustainable and renewable energy sources. The carbon emissions associated with mining have prompted concerns about Bitcoin's contribution to climate change and environmental degradation. The high energy consumption can also lead to high transaction fees, hindering Bitcoin's potential as a scalable and cost-effective payment system.

Several initiatives have emerged to address the energy consumption and environmental concerns of Bitcoin mining. A few mining companies have begun to switch to renewable energy in an effort to lower their carbon emissions. Mining pools are also looking into ways to utilize extra renewable energy that would otherwise be wasted. Such efforts aim to make Bitcoin mining more environmentally friendly and sustainable.

As the energy consumption and environmental impact of Bitcoin mining continue to be hotly debated, several alternative consensus mechanisms have gained traction as potential solutions. Proof of Stake (PoS) is one alternative that requires validators to put up a certain number of coins as collateral to create new blocks and validate transactions. PoS does not require resource-intensive mining, making it more energy-efficient and environmentally friendly than PoW.

Because proof of stake has the ability to lower energy usage and carbon emissions, it has becoming more and more popular. With the release of Ethereum 2.0, the second-largest cryptocurrency in the world, PoW is now being replaced with PoS. This transition addresses scalability and energy efficiency concerns, potentially making Ethereum a more sustainable and environmentally friendly blockchain network.

PoS offers several advantages over PoW regarding energy consumption and environmental impact. Firstly, PoS does not require miners to solve complex mathematical puzzles, significantly eliminating the need for resource-intensive mining hardware and reducing energy consumption. Secondly, PoS promotes decentralization by allowing anyone with coins to participate in the validation process, unlike PoW, where only miners with substantial computational power can effectively participate. Thirdly, PoS reduces the potential for centralization, as validators are selected depending on the number of coins they are willing to "stake," rather than their computational power.

While PoS addresses some of the energy consumption and environmental concerns associated with PoW, it also faces its challenges. One primary concern is the "rich-get- richer" problem, where validators with a significant stake in the network have a higher chance of being selected to create new blocks and receive rewards. This concentration of wealth and power could lead to centralization, undermining the decentralized nature of blockchain networks. Additionally, PoS introduces a potential attack vector, known as the "nothing-at-stake" problem, where validators may attempt to create multiple competing chains and double-spend without the same resource costs associated with PoW.

Addressing the energy consumption and environmental concerns of Bitcoin mining requires striking a balance between the security and decentralization offered by PoW and the energy efficiency and inclusivity of PoS. Some argue that transitioning to PoS may compromise the security and immutability of blockchain networks. However, others see PoS as a viable solution to make blockchain technology more sustainable and scalable while maintaining high security.

As blockchain technology continues to evolve, the debate between PoW and PoS, along with other consensus mechanisms, will shape the future of blockchain networks. Energy consumption and environmental considerations will play a crucial role in guiding the development of consensus mechanisms that are both secure and sustainable. Striking a balance between security, energy efficiency, and decentralization will be essential in creating blockchain networks that can meet the needs of diverse use cases while minimizing their environmental impact.

CHAPTER IV

The Bitcoin Network

Nodes and their role in the network

In the world of Bitcoin, nodes play a pivotal role in maintaining the decentralized and trustless nature of the network. As the backbone of the Bitcoin system, nodes form a distributed network that validates transactions, relays information, and ensures the security and integrity of the blockchain. In this section, we delve into the fundamental aspects of nodes, exploring their function, significance, and critical role in the seamless operation of the Bitcoin network.

At its core, a node in the Bitcoin network is a computer running the Bitcoin software, known as a full node. These full nodes maintain a complete copy of the entire Bitcoin blockchain, which contains a record of all transactions since the network's inception. Each full node independently verifies the validity of transactions and blocks, ensuring network consensus and preventing malicious or fraudulent activities.

One of the key functions of nodes is transaction validation. When a Bitcoin user initiates a transaction, it is broadcasted to the network, where the various nodes pick it up. Full nodes then verify the transaction against the rules defined by the Bitcoin protocol, ensuring that the transaction meets the necessary requirements and is valid. This verification process involves checking the digital signatures, ensuring sufficient funds, and confirming that the transaction adheres to the network's rules.

Nodes also play a crucial role in propagating information throughout the Bitcoin network. When a new transaction or block is validated and accepted by a node, it is immediately relayed to other nodes in the network. This rapid dissemination of information ensures that all nodes stay updated with the latest state of the blockchain, promoting network efficiency and synchronicity.

Furthermore, the Bitcoin network's general security and resilience are enhanced by the nodes' interconnectedness. With thousands of nodes distributed across the globe, Bitcoin becomes resistant to single points of failure and attacks. This decentralized nature makes it challenging for any single entity or group to manipulate or control the network, enhancing the trustworthiness and reliability of Bitcoin as a digital currency.

Running a full node comes with specific responsibilities and requirements. As full nodes maintain a complete copy of the blockchain, they require significant storage space to store the entire transaction history. Additionally, they demand processing power to validate transactions and participate in the consensus mechanism. Despite these resource requirements, many individuals and organizations choose to run full nodes to contribute to the network's decentralization and security.

However, not all nodes in the Bitcoin network are full nodes. Lightweight nodes, or simplified payment verification (SPV) nodes, are an alternative type of node that does not store the entire blockchain. These nodes rely on full nodes to perform transaction validation and only keep a limited data set, making them more suitable for devices with limited resources, such as mobile phones. While lightweight nodes offer reduced resource requirements, they rely on full nodes for transaction verification, making them slightly less secure than full nodes.

Beyond their technical functions, nodes also contribute to the governance and decision-making processes of the Bitcoin network. Major protocol upgrades or changes require consensus among the nodes to be implemented. If a significant portion of the network does not agree with a proposed change, it may result in a contentious hard fork, creating a separate blockchain.

Through their participation in the consensus mechanism, nodes work collectively to achieve agreement on the state of the blockchain. Through the procedure of mining, where miners compete to solve challenging mathematical puzzles, this consensus is obtained. In addition to receiving freshly created Bitcoins and transaction fees, the first miner to solve the puzzle obtains to add a new block of transactions to the blockchain.

Mining nodes play a specialized role in the network, as they create new blocks and secure the network through the proof-of-work mechanism. These mining nodes engage in resource-intensive computations to find a nonce that meets the difficulty requirement, thus proving that they have invested computational power in securing the network. As mining is a competitive process, miners must continuously expend resources to be the next one to add a block to the blockchain.

However, the increasing competitiveness of mining has led to the concentration of mining power in a few large mining pools. This concentration raises concerns about potential centralization and control over the network.

Some argue that this concentration may undermine the decentralized nature of Bitcoin, as a few entities can exert significant influence over the network's operations.

In response to this concern, alternative consensus mechanisms, such as proof-of-stake (PoS), have been proposed and implemented in various cryptocurrencies. Proof-of-stake does not rely on resource-intensive mining but instead on "staking" coins as collateral to participate in the consensus process. This approach addresses the energy consumption and centralization concerns associated with proof-of-work.

Bitcoin wallets and their types

Bitcoin wallets play a crucial role in cryptocurrency, serving as digital repositories where users can store, send, and receive their bitcoins. These wallets come in various forms, each offering unique features, security levels, and accessibility options. In this section, we will explore the significance of Bitcoin wallets, their role in the cryptocurrency ecosystem, and the different types of wallets available to users.

At the core of Bitcoin wallets are cryptographic keys, consisting of private and public keys, which facilitate secure transactions on the blockchain. Unlike traditional wallets that hold physical cash and cards, Bitcoin wallets are software applications or hardware devices that allow users to engage with the Bitcoin network, managing their digital assets.

Bitcoin wallets fulfill several essential functions within the cryptocurrency ecosystem. They serve as the means to store and safeguard users' funds and enable the seamless transfer of bitcoins to other wallet addresses.

Additionally, wallets keep track of users' transaction histories, allowing them to monitor their balances and transaction activity.

The different types of Bitcoin wallets cater to various user preferences and security requirements. Software wallets are the most common and are available in multiple forms. Desktop wallets run on personal computers or laptops, offering higher security by storing private keys locally. Mobile wallets, designed for smartphones and tablets, provide convenience and accessibility on the go, but may expose users to more security risks if the device is compromised. Online wallets operate on cloud servers and can be accessed via web browsers, offering convenience but potentially exposing private keys to third-party control.

In contrast, hardware wallets are physical devices specifically designed to store private keys securely. These wallets keep the keys offline, reducing the risk of cyberattacks, and provide enhanced security during transactions by remaining disconnected from the internet. Popular hardware wallet brands such as Ledger and Trezor have gained widespread adoption due to their robust security features.

For those seeking an offline cold storage solution, paper wallets can print private and public keys on a physical document. While paper wallets are considered secure when generated and stored correctly, users must exercise caution to prevent physical damage or theft of the paper containing their keys.

An interesting and less common type of wallet is the brain wallet, where the user's private keys are derived from a passphrase or sequence of words memorized by the user. This unique approach removes the need for physical storage, but users must be cautious to choose a strong passphrase to prevent potential brute-force attacks.

When choosing a Bitcoin wallet, users must consider several factors. Security is of utmost importance, and those seeking the highest level of protection may opt for hardware wallets or certain types of software wallets. Convenience and accessibility are also crucial, with mobile and online wallets offering easy access to funds, albeit with varying degrees of security.

Users should prioritize backup and recovery options to safeguard their funds. Some wallets offer seed phrases that can be used to restore the wallet on a new device in case of device loss or failure.

Transaction fees can also vary depending on the wallet type and service provider, so users should consider transaction costs associated with sending and receiving bitcoins.

Despite the secure nature of Bitcoin wallets, they are not immune to risks. Software wallets and online wallets may be vulnerable to cyberattacks, such as hacking or phishing attempts, leading to the loss of funds. Hardware wallets and paper wallets can be susceptible to physical damage, loss, or theft, potentially resulting in the loss of access to funds.

Users can follow best practices to enhance wallet security, such as using hardware wallets to keep private keys offline and enabling two-factor authentication (2FA) for additional security. Properly creating secure backups and keeping software up-to-date are also essential practices to safeguard funds and protect against known vulnerabilities.

Transactions and confirmations

Bitcoin, the pioneering cryptocurrency introduced by Satoshi Nakamoto in 2009, revolutionized how we perceive and transact with money. At the heart of the Bitcoin network lies its transaction system, allowing users to transfer value across the globe without the need for intermediaries. In this section, we delve into the intricacies of Bitcoin transactions, exploring how they work, the role of transaction confirmations, and the mechanisms that underpin the security and efficiency of the network.

Bitcoin transactions are the fundamental units of value transfer within the network. They enable users to send and receive bitcoins to and from various addresses on the blockchain. A Bitcoin transaction consists of inputs, outputs, and a digital signature. Inputs represent the bitcoins being spent, while outputs signify the new ownership of these bitcoins. The digital signature provides cryptographic proof that the owner of the sending address authorizes the transaction.

When users initiate a Bitcoin transaction, they create a digital message containing the necessary details, such as the recipient's address and the amount of bitcoins being sent. The transaction message is then broadcasted to the Bitcoin network, where it becomes visible to other nodes and miners. Miners are the one responsible for validating transactions and adding them to new blocks on the blockchain.

Initially, a transaction is unconfirmed and resides in the mempool, a temporary storage area for transactions that are pending. Here, miners select transactions they wish to include in the next block based on transaction fees and size. Unconfirmed transactions are vulnerable to double-spending attempts, where a malicious user attempts to use the same bitcoins twice. To mitigate this risk, Bitcoin's consensus mechanism plays a crucial role.

Confirmation is when a Bitcoin transaction becomes permanently recorded on the blockchain. Each new block added to the blockchain contains a set of confirmed transactions. As the blockchain grows, the number of blocks added after a particular transaction increases, enhancing the confidence in its validity.

Bitcoin employs a PoW consensus mechanism to achieve transaction confirmation. When miners successfully solve complex mathematical puzzles through PoW, they earn the right to create new blocks and include a set of transactions into the blockchain, including the one they confirmed. As more blocks are added on top of a transaction's block, the transaction gains more confirmations, making it increasingly difficult to reverse.

Confirmations are essential to ensure the validity and security of Bitcoin transactions. As more confirmations accumulate, the likelihood of a transaction being altered or reversed decreases significantly. For small-value transactions, one or two confirmations may suffice. However, more confirmations are advisable for higher-value transactions to reduce the risk of double-spending attempts.

Miners prioritize transactions with higher fees, receiving them as rewards for adding transactions to blocks. Consequently, transactions with higher fees will likely be included in blocks sooner and receive confirmations faster. Users can choose their desired transaction fee, which directly impacts the speed at which their transactions are confirmed.

Double spending is a concern in decentralized digital currencies like Bitcoin, where a central authority does not control transactions. Unconfirmed transactions, in particular, are susceptible to double-spending attempts, as the spender may attempt to broadcast two conflicting transactions simultaneously. For this reason, recipients often wait for transaction confirmations before accepting payments, especially for higher-value transactions.

Bitcoin's block time, the average time it takes to mine a new block, is approximately 10 minutes. This means that, on average, a transaction can take 10 minutes to receive its first confirmation. However, confirmation times can vary based on factors such as network congestion and transaction fees. During times of high network activity, transaction fees may rise, prompting users to prioritize their transactions with higher fees for faster confirmations.

Zero-confirmation transactions refer to transactions that have been broadcasted to the network but have not yet received any confirmations. While zero-confirmation transactions are faster, they are less secure than transactions with multiple confirmations. Merchants and businesses often accept zero-confirmation transactions for low-value purchases but may require additional confirmations for larger transactions.

Zero-confirmation transactions carry a risk of double-spending, making them less suitable for high-value purchases. In a double-spending attack, a malicious actor could send two conflicting transactions simultaneously, trying to spend the same bitcoins in different places. For this reason, zero-confirmation transactions are generally not recommended for transactions involving significant sums.

Transaction fees serve as incentives for miners to prioritize certain transactions over others. When users include higher transaction fees, miners will pick up their transactions and include them in the next block. Conversely, lower-fee transactions may experience delays in confirmation, especially during periods of high network congestion.

Some Bitcoin mining pools offer transaction accelerators, a service that allows users to speed up the confirmation of their transactions. Users can submit their transaction ID to the accelerator, and if the pool accepts it, the transaction gets included in the next block mined by that pool.

SegWit is a protocol upgrade that addresses transaction malleability, a previously existing issue in Bitcoin. Transaction malleability allowed attackers to modify the digital signature of a transaction, resulting in a new transaction ID. This malleability complicated the tracking of transaction confirmations and made specific improvements, such as the Lightning Network, more challenging to implement.

Lightning Network is a second-layer solution created on top of the Bitcoin blockchain that aims to enable faster and cheaper transactions. It achieves this by creating payment channels between users, allowing them to conduct off-chain transactions without the need for confirmations. The Lightning Network significantly improves transaction scalability and enables near-instant payments while alleviating the burden on the main blockchain.

CHAPTER V

Bitcoin's Monetary Policy

Fixed supply and scarcity

Ever since its launch in 2009, Bitcoin has emerged as a groundbreaking digital currency, challenging traditional financial systems and reshaping how we perceive and interact with money. One of the most intriguing and critical aspects of Bitcoin is its fixed supply and inherent scarcity. Unlike fiat currencies that central authorities can print at will, Bitcoin has a predetermined limit of 21 million coins, making it deflationary and highly sought after for its potential to act as digital gold.

The fixed supply of Bitcoin is not a coincidence but rather a fundamental design feature built into its underlying protocol. Satoshi Nakamoto, the anonymous creator of Bitcoin, specified this scarcity as a way to mimic the characteristics of precious metals like gold. Like gold, whose supply is limited and finite, Bitcoin's fixed supply ensures that no new coins can be created beyond the established 21 million cap.

To maintain its network and validate transactions, Bitcoin relies on a process called mining, which involves solving complex mathematical puzzles through the Proof-of-Work (PoW) consensus mechanism. In exchange for their efforts and computational power, miners are rewarded with new bitcoins, which act as block rewards for confirming transactions and securing the network.

However, this block reward is not static but undergoes periodic reductions known as halving events.

The Bitcoin network undergoes a halving event approximately every four years, where the block reward is cut in half. Initially set at 50 bitcoins, the block reward has been halved multiple times, reducing it to 25, 12.5, and so on. This halving process creates a diminishing rate of new bitcoin issuance, effectively slowing down the rate at which new bitcoins are introduced into circulation. It also contributes to the scarcity of the cryptocurrency.

The scarcity of Bitcoin and its fixed supply have significant implications for its price and value in the market. As demand for Bitcoin increases and its supply remains limited, basic economic principles suggest that its price should rise over time. This phenomenon is often referred to as the stock-to-flow model, which measures the ratio of the existing supply (stock) to a commodity's new production (flow). A higher stock-to-flow ratio signifies greater scarcity, potentially leading to higher prices.

The stock-to-flow model has garnered attention from economists and investors, who see Bitcoin as a store of value akin to gold. Gold has a high stock-to-flow ratio, contributing to its status as a reliable store of wealth and a hedge against economic uncertainties. Similarly, Bitcoin's scarcity and fixed supply make it increasingly attractive to those seeking a digital asset with properties similar to precious metals.

This concept of scarcity and its potential to preserve wealth has given rise to the phenomenon of "hodling" within the Bitcoin community. Hodling, derived from a misspelling of the word "holding," refers to the practice of holding onto bitcoins for the long term, with the belief that the cryptocurrency's value will appreciate over time. The scarcity of Bitcoin is seen as a key factor supporting this long-term investment strategy.

In contrast to Bitcoin's fixed supply, fiat currencies issued by central banks are subject to inflation, a process where the money supply increases over time, leading to a decrease in the currency's purchasing power. Central banks can print money at will to meet economic objectives, but this practice also poses the risk of devaluing the currency. In contrast, Bitcoin's fixed supply ensures that its value cannot be eroded through excessive issuance, providing a hedge against inflationary pressures.

However, the scarcity and fixed supply of Bitcoin also raise concerns about potential deflationary pressures in the economy. In traditional economic systems, mild inflation is generally considered healthy for stimulating spending and economic growth. Conversely, deflation can lead to a preference for saving and hoarding, potentially reducing economic activity. Critics argue that this deflationary nature may hinder Bitcoin's broader adoption as a medium of exchange.

Bitcoin's scarcity is not without its challenges, as forks and the rise of alternative cryptocurrencies pose potential threats to its uniqueness. Forks can create new versions of Bitcoin, potentially diluting its scarcity and diverting demand to other digital assets. Additionally, the growth of other cryptocurrencies with its supply mechanisms may introduce competition to Bitcoin's status as the preeminent scarce digital asset.

Nevertheless, Bitcoin's fixed supply and inherent scarcity remain integral to its value proposition and have played a crucial role in the cryptocurrency's journey from obscurity to global recognition. The rise of digital gold and the growing adoption of Bitcoin as a store of value demonstrates the significance of scarcity in the minds of investors and the broader public. As cryptocurrency matures and evolves, its fixed supply will remain a defining characteristic, shaping its role in the global financial landscape and its potential to disrupt traditional economic paradigms.

The halving events and their significance

Ever since its launch in 2009, Bitcoin has transformed the world of finance, introducing a decentralized digital currency that runs outside the control of traditional financial institutions. At the core of Bitcoin's monetary policy lies a unique and crucial feature known as halving events. In this section, we delve into the concept of halving, its historical significance, the rationale behind its implementation, and the potential implications these events may hold for the future of Bitcoin.

Halving, also known as "halvening," is an essential aspect of Bitcoin's protocol that affects the issuance rate of new bitcoins. The process involves cutting the block reward in half approximately every four years. When Bitcoin first launched, miners received a block reward of 50 bitcoins for each successfully mined block. The first halving event, which took place in 2012, reduced the block reward to 25 bitcoins. Subsequent halvings in 2016 and 2020 further reduced the reward to 12.5 and 6.25 bitcoins, respectively.

The concept of halving is rooted in Bitcoin's design philosophy and monetary policy. Satoshi Nakamoto, the unknown creator of Bitcoin, intended to create a deflationary digital currency that would mimic the scarcity of valuable metals like gold. By reducing the rate of new bitcoin issuance over time, halving events gradually slow down the creation of new bitcoins until the total supply reaches the predetermined cap of 21 million coins. This deliberate reduction in issuance stands in comparison with traditional fiat currencies, which can be printed without bounds, leading to inflation and decreased purchasing power over time.

Each halving event in Bitcoin's history has marked a significant milestone in the cryptocurrency's journey. The first halving in 2012 served as a critical test, demonstrating the viability of Bitcoin's monetary policy and the resilience of its network. The second halving in 2016 saw Bitcoin's popularity grow exponentially, attracting more users, investors, and businesses into the ecosystem. The most recent halving in 2020 occurred amidst a backdrop of increasing institutional interest in Bitcoin, further solidifying its position as a store of value and a potential hedge against economic uncertainties.

Halving events have profound implications for Bitcoin miners, the participants responsible for validating transactions and securing the network. With the block reward being cut in half, miners receive fewer bitcoins as rewards for their efforts. This reduction in revenue can put significant pressure on miners, especially those operating with higher costs or less efficient hardware. Some miners may find it economically unviable to continue their operations post-halving, leading to potential shifts in the distribution of mining power and the overall network hashrate.

The anticipation and occurrence of halving events often trigger significant market speculation and impact Bitcoin's price dynamics. Historically, halvings have been associated with bull markets and price surges. The reduction in new bitcoin issuance leads to a decrease in the selling pressure from miners, potentially creating a supply-demand imbalance that favors higher prices. The expectation of scarcity and the possibility of a "halving pump" have attracted investors seeking to capitalize on potential price rallies.

The "hodling" concept derived from a misspelling of the word "holding" has become synonymous with Bitcoin culture. Hodlers hold onto their bitcoins for the long term, confident in the cryptocurrency's potential for appreciation over time. Halving events reinforce this investment strategy, as the reduced issuance rate is seen as a signal for potential price appreciation. The concept of hodling has become a defining characteristic of Bitcoin's community, embodying the belief in the cryptocurrency's long-term value proposition.

Halving events also play a significant role in shaping Bitcoin's scarcity and its stock-to-flow model. As the issuance rate decreases with each halving, the stock-to-flow ratio of Bitcoin increases, making it scarcer over time. The stock-to-flow model, which measures the ratio of the existing supply to the new production (flow), has been used to predict Bitcoin's price trajectory and has gained popularity as an analytical tool for understanding the cryptocurrency's market behavior.

While halving events may impact miners' revenue, they also reinforce the security of the Bitcoin network. Miners are incentivized to prioritize transaction fees to sustain their profitability as the block reward decreases. This change aligns with Bitcoin's long-term vision, where transaction fees are expected to become the main incentive for miners once the block reward eventually diminishes to zero.

Halving events have a profound psychological impact on market sentiment, influencing investor perceptions and driving media attention. The anticipation of a halving event often leads to a period of heightened speculation and price volatility. Media coverage intensifies, attracting new interest from both retail and institutional investors. The increased attention can spur adoption, investment, and further development within the Bitcoin ecosystem.

Looking ahead, three remaining halving events are scheduled to occur at roughly four-year intervals, leading up to the year 2140 when the maximum supply of 21 million bitcoins will be reached. Each halving will further reduce the rate of new bitcoin issuance, making it increasingly difficult and rare to obtain new coins. The impact of these future halvings on Bitcoin's price, adoption, and network dynamics remains a topic of keen interest and speculation within the cryptocurrency community.

Comparisons to traditional fiat currencies

In the realm of global finance, Bitcoin has emerged as a disruptor, challenging the long-established dominance of traditional fiat currencies issued by central banks and governments. Bitcoin offers a unique and innovative alternative to the conventional financial system. In this section, we explore the key comparisons between Bitcoin and traditional fiat currencies, examining the fundamental differences and implications for the future of money and value exchange.

One of the most striking distinctions between Bitcoin and traditional fiat currencies is their issuance and control mechanisms. Fiat currencies are created and regulated by central banks and governments. These institutions can issue new currency units and manage monetary policies to control inflation, interest rates, and economic stability. On the other hand, Bitcoin operates on a decentralized network, and its issuance is governed by a pre-defined algorithm, known as the Bitcoin protocol. This fixed supply of 21 million coins ensures that Bitcoin's issuance is predictable and not subject to the whims of central authorities.

The fixed supply and scarcity of Bitcoin have contributed to its appeal as a potential store of value. Unlike fiat currencies that may be susceptible to inflationary pressures and depreciating purchasing power over time, Bitcoin's scarcity implies that its value could appreciate over the long term. This characteristic has attracted investors seeking a hedge against inflation and financial instability, viewing Bitcoin as a digital counterpart to traditional safe-haven assets like gold.

Transaction speed and cost represent another significant comparison between Bitcoin and traditional fiat currencies. Traditional banking systems often involve intermediaries, such as banks and payment processors, leading to delays and additional fees in cross-border transactions. On the other hand, Bitcoin operates on a peer-to-peer network, allowing for faster and borderless transactions without intermediaries. While Bitcoin transactions can offer quicker settlement times, the problem of scalability and high transaction fees during peak periods remains a challenge that the cryptocurrency community continues to address.

One of the fundamental appeals of Bitcoin is its ability to facilitate financial inclusion, especially in regions with insufficient access to traditional banking services. Approximately 1.7 billion people globally remain unbanked, with limited access to financial tools and services. Bitcoin's decentralized nature enables anyone with an internet to access and partake in the network, offering an alternative financial system to those excluded from traditional banking services.

Furthermore, Bitcoin provides a potential solution for remittances, which are costly and time-consuming for individuals sending money across borders. Traditional remittance services often involve hefty fees, making it expensive for individuals to transfer funds to family and friends in other countries. Bitcoin's borderless nature allows for faster and more cost-effective cross-border remittances, enabling people to send money internationally with reduced fees and faster processing times.

However, it is essential to acknowledge that Bitcoin's comparisons to traditional fiat currencies also reveal several limitations and challenges. One of the primary concerns is its price volatility. Bitcoin's value is known for experiencing significant fluctuations, making it challenging for everyday transactions and store-of-value purposes. The potential for rapid price swings can also deter merchants from accepting Bitcoin as a payment method, as they may face uncertainty about the currency's purchasing power.

Additionally, the lack of regulatory oversight in cryptocurrency has raised concerns regarding consumer protection, fraud, and money laundering risks. Traditional banking systems are subject to strict regulatory frameworks to ensure financial stability and protect consumers. However, the decentralized and pseudonymous nature of Bitcoin makes it challenging to trace and regulate transactions, leading to debates about striking a balance between fostering innovation and implementing appropriate regulations.

The scalability issue is another noteworthy consideration in comparing Bitcoin to traditional fiat currencies. As the number of Bitcoin users and transactions grows, the network faces challenges in processing more transactions within a reasonable timeframe. This concern has prompted discussions and efforts to develop scaling solutions to enhance Bitcoin's transaction throughput and user experience.

The environmental impact of Bitcoin mining has also garnered attention, with concerns about the significant energy consumption required for proof-of-work mining. The energy-intensive nature of mining has led to discussions about its carbon footprint and potential environmental implications. As the world focuses on sustainability and reducing greenhouse gas emissions, finding energy-efficient mining alternatives or transitioning to alternative consensus mechanisms like proof-of-stake becomes a subject of interest and debate.

CHAPTER VI

Security and Privacy in Bitcoin

Cryptographic principles behind Bitcoin's security

Bitcoin, the pioneering cryptocurrency that sparked a financial revolution, relies on a sophisticated combination of cryptographic principles to ensure its security, transparency, and decentralization. Introduced by an anonymous entity known as Satoshi Nakamoto in 2009, Bitcoin's innovative design incorporates cryptographic techniques that underpin its fundamental security features. In this section, we delve into the cryptographic principles behind Bitcoin's security, exploring key concepts such as hashing, digital signatures, public- private key pairs, and the consensus mechanism known as Proof-of-Work.

At the heart of Bitcoin's security lies the concept of hashing. Hashing is a one-way function that takes an input (known as the message) and produces a fixed-size output known as the hash. The beauty of hashing lies in its properties: it is deterministic, which means that the same input will always create the same hash, and it is computationally impossible to reverse-engineer the original input from the hash. This one-way nature of hashing is crucial in securing Bitcoin's blockchain, the distributed ledger that records all transactions.

In Bitcoin, each block contains a list of transactions, and a cryptographic hash is generated for the entire block. This hash is then used as a reference, or "pointer," to the previous block's hash, effectively linking the blocks together in a chain. Any alteration to the data within a block will result in a completely different hash, breaking the chain and invalidating subsequent blocks. As a result, the tamper-resistant nature of hashing ensures the immutability of the blockchain, safeguarding the integrity of transaction history.

Another essential cryptographic principle in Bitcoin's security arsenal is using digital signatures. Digital signatures allow users to prove ownership of their private keys and authorize transactions without revealing sensitive information. Digital signatures consist of two components: a private key, known only to the owner, and a corresponding public key, which is openly shared.

When a user initiates a Bitcoin transaction, the transaction details are combined with the user's private key and hashed. This hash is then encrypted by utilizing the private key, resulting in a digital signature. The signature is appended to the transaction data and broadcasted to the network. Other participants can verify the transaction's authenticity by utilizing the sender's public key to decrypt the signature, obtaining the original hash, and comparing it to the hash of the transaction data. If the two hashes match, the transaction is considered valid.

Digital signatures guarantee the integrity and authenticity of Bitcoin transactions, preventing unauthorized parties from manipulating or impersonating transactions on the network. They play a crucial role in maintaining the security and trustworthiness of the decentralized Bitcoin ecosystem.

The cryptographic principles behind Bitcoin's security also leverage the concept of public-private key pairs. Each user in the Bitcoin network possesses a pair of cryptographic keys: a public key, which is openly shared with others, and a private key, which must be kept secret. The two keys are mathematically linked, enabling data encrypted with one key to be decrypted only by its corresponding key in the pair.

Public-private key pairs play a pivotal role in securing Bitcoin addresses and transactions. A Bitcoin address is a cryptographic representation of a user's public key, serving as the destination for incoming transactions. When sending bitcoins, the sender references the recipient's address and uses their public key to encrypt the transaction details. The recipient, in turn, utilizes their private key to decrypt the transaction and gain access to the received bitcoins.

The strength of public-private key cryptography lies in the computational infeasibility of deriving a private key from its associated public key. This property ensures the security of Bitcoin addresses and prevents unauthorized parties from accessing funds belonging to other users.

Bitcoin's consensus mechanism, known as Proof-of-Work (PoW), is a cryptographic process that plays a vital role in maintaining the safety and decentralization of the network. PoW is a process in which miners compete to solve a computationally challenging mathematical puzzle. The first miner to find the solution for the puzzle is granted the right to create and add a new block to the blockchain. This process is energy-intensive and requires substantial computational power, making it difficult for any single entity to dominate the network.

The puzzle-solving process in PoW involves repeatedly hashing the block's data with a randomly generated number until a specific pattern, called the "nonce," is found. The successful miner broadcasts the solution to the network, and other participants verify the solution's validity. The miner receives freshly created bitcoins and transaction fees if their solution is accurate, and the new block is uploaded to the blockchain.

PoW serves as a mechanism to achieve consensus in a decentralized network. As most miners compete to find the next block, they effectively confirm the validity of the entire blockchain up to that point. Attempting to alter past transactions or insert fraudulent information into the blockchain would require an astronomical amount of computational power, making the system incredibly secure against attacks.

While Bitcoin's cryptographic principles have proven to be robust and effective, there are still potential challenges and security implications to consider. As Bitcoin's popularity continues to grow, the computational power required for mining has increased significantly, leading to concerns about the impact of PoW in the environment. Efforts are underway to explore alternative consensus mechanisms, such as Proof-of-Stake (PoS), which offer energy-efficient alternatives to PoW. PoS relies on validators who "stake" their coins as collateral to confirm transactions and create new blocks, eliminating the need for intensive computational puzzles. While PoS has its merits, it presents different security considerations and trade-offs compared to PoW.

Moreover, the security of Bitcoin ultimately relies on the strength of the cryptographic algorithms used. As technology advances, it becomes essential to ensure that the cryptographic methods employed remain resistant to attacks and exploits. Regular upgrades and scrutiny of the cryptographic protocols are necessary to maintain Bitcoin's robustness against potential threats.

Public and private keys

In the realm of modern cryptography, public and private keys are the cornerstones of secure communication and authentication. These cryptographic key pairs play a crucial role in ensuring digital information's confidentiality, integrity, and authenticity. Introduced in the late 1970s as part of asymmetric encryption, public and private keys revolutionized how we transmit sensitive data and communicate online.

At the heart of asymmetric encryption lies the idea that information encrypted with the public key can only be decrypted by utilizing the corresponding private key, and vice versa. The public key, openly shared, serves as the encryption key, while the private key, held securely, is the decryption key. This two-key system provides a robust method for secure communication between parties without the need for prior exchange of secret keys.

The use of public and private keys has profound implications for secure communication. In scenarios where confidentiality is paramount, the sender can encrypt sensitive data using the recipient's public key, guaranteeing that only the intended recipient can decrypt and access the information. This process prevents eavesdroppers or malicious actors from intercepting and understanding the encrypted message, providing a strong defense against data breaches and unauthorized access.

Beyond encryption, public and private keys also play a vital role in authentication through digital signatures. A digital signature is generated by hashing a message and encrypting the resulting hash with the sender's private key. The encrypted hash and the original message constitute the digital signature. The recipient can verify the authenticity as well as integrity of the message by decrypting the signature with the sender's public key and comparing it to the recalculated hash of the message. Digital signatures ensure that messages are tamper-proof and come from the expected sender, guarding against impersonation and ensuring data integrity.

The security of public and private keys is rooted in complex mathematical algorithms. Creating key pairs involves sophisticated mathematical processes that make it computationally infeasible to derive the private key from the public key. This mathematical unforgeability ensures that the secrecy of the private key remains intact, even when the public key is openly shared.

Key generation and management are critical aspects of cryptographic security. The randomness and unpredictability of key generation are crucial to prevent brute force attacks, where an attacker systematically tries every possible key combination to decrypt encrypted data. Cryptographic key management involves securely storing private keys and distributing public keys to trusted parties, safeguarding the integrity and confidentiality of the keys.

The length of cryptographic keys significantly impacts their security. Longer key lengths provide higher levels of security but may come with increased computational overhead for encryption and decryption processes. As computing power advances, longer key lengths become necessary to maintain the same level of security.
Public and private keys are at the heart of various secure communication protocols used on the internet. One

notable example is the Secure Sockets Layer (SSL)/Transport Layer Security (TLS) protocol, utilized to protect data transfer between servers and web browsers. In TLS, the server presents a certificate containing its public key, which the browser uses to encrypt and establish a secure connection. This process ensures that data exchanged during the session is encrypted and protected from interception, preventing unauthorized access to sensitive information.

While public and private keys have revolutionized secure communication, they are not immune to potential risks and challenges. Key management, including key generation, storage, and distribution, remains critical to cryptographic security. Compromising a private key can have devastating consequences, including unauthorized access, data breaches, and digital impersonation.

Quantum computing presents a unique challenge to traditional asymmetric encryption methods. Quantum computers have the potential to break specific encryption algorithms, necessitating the exploration of quantum-resistant encryption methods to safeguard the future of cryptographic security.

Best practices for securing Bitcoin holdings

Given the growing acceptance of cryptocurrencies such as Bitcoin, securing digital assets has become a paramount concern for investors and users alike. Bitcoin's decentralized and irreversible nature makes it imperative for individuals to adopt robust security practices to safeguard their holdings from threats such as hacking, phishing, and theft. In this section, we explore the best practices for securing Bitcoin holdings, covering various aspects of wallet management, hardware wallets, multi-factor authentication, and the importance of staying vigilant in an ever-evolving digital landscape.

The first step in securing Bitcoin holdings is understanding the concept of a Bitcoin wallet. A digital container used to store private keys necessary for managing and accessing Bitcoin funds is called a wallet. Differentiating between the two primary types of wallets—hot and cold—is crucial. Hot wallets are the best option for frequent transactions and accessibility because they are internet-connected. However, they are more vulnerable to potential online threats. On the other hand, cold wallets are offline and provide enhanced security as they are not exposed to the internet. Using a combination of both types is crucial to balance accessibility and security.

Selecting a reputable and secure Bitcoin wallet is critical for safeguarding holdings. Various wallet options are available, including online wallets, mobile wallets, desktop wallets, and hardware wallets. Online and mobile wallets are convenient for quick transactions but require stringent security measures and regular updates to protect against potential attacks. Desktop wallets offer better security than online and mobile wallets as they are less exposed to online threats. However, it is essential to use reputable and regularly updated desktop wallets to ensure the highest level of protection. Hardware wallets, often considered the gold standard in Bitcoin security, offer an offline and highly secure method of storing private keys. These physical devices store private keys and sign transactions offline, providing additional protection against online threats. Hardware wallets are resistant to computer viruses and malware, making them an ideal choice for long-term Bitcoin holdings.

Multi-factor authentication (MFA) is a vital security practice that adds protection to Bitcoin holdings. MFA requires users to give multiple forms of identification before gaining access to their wallets. This could include a combination of something they know (like a password), something they have (like a hardware wallet or mobile device), and something they are (like a biometric identifier). By implementing MFA, users ensure that their Bitcoin holdings remain secure even if one factor is compromised. MFA is widely available on various wallet platforms and is highly recommended for all users seeking to enrich the security of their digital assets.

Keeping a software and firmware updated is fundamental to maintaining the security of Bitcoin holdings. Developers continually release updates to address potential vulnerabilities and enhance security measures. Neglecting to update wallet software or firmware may expose holdings to known threats that could have been prevented with timely updates. Regularly updating wallet software and firmware is especially crucial for online and desktop wallets, as they are more susceptible to online threats. While more secure due to their offline nature, hardware wallets should also be updated when new firmware releases are available to ensure ongoing protection against potential exploits.

Strong passwords and backup phrases are essential for protecting Bitcoin holdings. When creating a password for a Bitcoin wallet, users should use a combination of an upper and a lowercase letters, numbers, and special characters to make it resistant to brute force attacks. Additionally, avoiding using easily guessable information such as names or birthdates is crucial. Backup phrases, also known as recovery seeds or mnemonics, are strings of words used to recover a wallet if the original device is lost or damaged. These phrases should be stored in a secure and offline location, known only to the wallet owner. A backup phrase acts as a fail-safe to regain access to Bitcoin holdings, emphasizing its importance in securing digital assets.

For users seeking an extra layer of protection, offline storage and paper wallets provide an air-gapped method of securing Bitcoin holdings. Paper wallets involve printing the private keys and QR codes on a physical piece of paper, which is then stored in a secure location away from internet-connected devices. Using paper wallets for long-term storage of significant Bitcoin holdings ensures that the private keys remain offline and away from potential online threats. However, users must exercise caution in securely generating and printing paper wallets, as any exposure of private keys during the process could compromise the security of the holdings.

Staying vigilant and skeptical is crucial in safeguarding Bitcoin holdings. Users should exercise caution when interacting with third-party services and always verify the authenticity of websites, applications, and wallet providers. Scammers and phishing attempts are prevalent in cryptocurrency, and users should be cautious about sharing personal information or private keys with unknown entities. Avoiding suspicious links, emails, or communications and conducting thorough research before using any new service or wallet provider can prevent falling victim to potential scams or security breaches.

Hardware wallets offer the added advantage of offline transaction signing, enhancing Bitcoin holdings' security. Offline transaction signing allows users to create and sign transactions on an offline device, such as a hardware wallet, and then broadcast the signed transaction to the Bitcoin network using an online device. By keeping the private keys offline during the transaction signing process, users can protect their holdings from potential online threats, ensuring the integrity and security of the transaction.

Regular security audits of Bitcoin wallets and storage methods are crucial to identifying potential vulnerabilities and weaknesses. Users should periodically review their security measures, update software and firmware, and conduct test transactions to ensure everything functions as expected. Additionally, users should check access logs and wallet activity to determine any unauthorized access or suspicious behavior. Regular security audits contribute to maintaining the highest level of security for Bitcoin holdings.

CHAPTER VII

Bitcoin Transactions and Fees

How transactions are structured

In cryptocurrencies, transactions form the backbone of decentralized financial systems. For Bitcoin and many other blockchain-based cryptocurrencies, understanding how transactions are structured is fundamental to grasping the underlying mechanics of these digital assets. In this section, we delve into the intricacies of transaction structures, exploring the key components, processes, and security considerations that make up the foundation of peer-to-peer cryptocurrency transfers.

A cryptocurrency transaction comprises several essential elements that work together to enable the transfer of value between participants. At its core, a transaction consists of inputs, outputs, and transaction fees. These components intertwine to create a transparent and immutable record of financial transfers.

Inputs represent the source of funds for a transaction. They consist of unspent transaction outputs (UTXOs) from previous transactions, essentially serving as the inputs used to initiate the current transaction. Each UTXO specifies the number of coins it holds and the recipient's address.

Outputs, however, represent the destinations for the funds being transferred. Each output specifies the amount of cryptocurrency to be sent and the recipient's address.

A single transaction can have multiple outputs, sending funds to multiple recipients simultaneously.

Transaction fees are a critical aspect of cryptocurrency transactions. As blockchain networks rely on miners or validators to verify and place transactions to the blockchain, fees incentivize these participants to include specific transactions in the next block. The higher the transaction fee, the more attractive the transaction becomes to miners, as they are more likely to prioritize transactions with higher fees due to the potential for increased rewards.

Before a transaction can be added to the blockchain, it must be cryptographically signed. Transaction signing ensures the authenticity and integrity of the transaction. When initiating a transaction, the sender signs it with their private key, proving ownership of the funds. Subsequently, the recipient can confirm that the transaction's signature hasn't been altered during transmission by using the sender's public key.

A transaction is given a distinct identification known as a transaction hash once it is signed and sent out to the network. This hash is a cryptographic representation of the transaction data, serving as a digital fingerprint that uniquely identifies the transaction. Users are able to monitor the progress of their transactions and confirm that they have been added to the blockchain by using the transaction hash as a point of reference.

After a transaction is broadcast to the network, it enters a pool of unconfirmed transactions known as the mempool. Miners select transactions from the mempool and include them in the next block they mine. As part of the mining process, miners compete to solve a complicated mathematical puzzle, with the first miner to solve it being rewarded with newly minted coins and transaction fees from the block.

Once a transaction is included in a block and placed to the blockchain, it is considered confirmed. The number of confirmations a transaction receives indicates the depth of its inclusion in the blockchain, with each new block added after the initial confirmation adding to the security and immutability of the transaction.

Privacy and security are essential considerations in transaction structures. While blockchain networks are often described as transparent due to their public nature, the details of individual transactions are not readily associated with users' identities. Instead, transactions are pseudonymous, identified only by addresses rather than personal information.

However, transaction privacy can be enhanced through various techniques such as using privacy-focused cryptocurrencies, employing coin-mixing services, or utilizing advanced cryptographic protocols like zero-knowledge proofs. These measures obscure the link between transaction inputs and outputs, further protecting user privacy.

The finality of cryptocurrency transactions is a crucial aspect for users and merchants. Once a transaction is confirmed and added to the blockchain, it becomes irreversible. Unlike traditional financial systems, where transactions can be reversed or disputed, blockchain transactions are immutable and permanent.

The finality of transactions provides security and certainty for merchants, as they can trust that it cannot be revoked once a payment is confirmed. However, it also underscores the importance of verifying transaction details before initiating a transfer, as errors or mistakes cannot be undone.

Transaction throughput and scalability are ongoing challenges for blockchain networks. One important performance indicator that directly affects a blockchain's usefulness for regular transactions and applications is the number of transactions it can manage per second.

Various scaling solutions, such as layer-two protocols like the Lightning Network for Bitcoin and sharding for Ethereum, aim to increase transaction throughput while maintaining the decentralized nature of blockchain networks. These solutions work to reduce congestion and improve transaction speeds, making cryptocurrencies more efficient and scalable for mass adoption.

Understanding how transactions are structured is vital for anyone involved in cryptocurrencies. Transactions form the backbone of blockchain networks, enabling peer-to-peer value transfers in a decentralized and secure manner. The interplay between inputs, outputs, transaction fees, signing, and confirmation processes creates a transparent and immutable record of financial transfers.

As the adoption of cryptocurrencies grows, the ongoing development of transaction privacy, finality, throughput, and scalability becomes essential. Advancements in blockchain technology and the exploration of innovative solutions are critical to making cryptocurrencies more efficient, secure, and accessible for users worldwide. By staying informed about transaction structures and the evolving landscape of blockchain networks, individuals can navigate the world of cryptocurrencies with confidence and security, harnessing the power of decentralized finance for a more inclusive financial future.

Transaction fees and their determinants

Bitcoin, the pioneering cryptocurrency, has experienced unprecedented growth and adoption since its inception. As the number of Bitcoin transactions increases, the need for efficient and timely processing becomes paramount. Transaction fees are crucial in incentivizing miners to include transactions in blocks and prioritize them based on their fee rates. In this section, we explore the intricacies of Bitcoin's transaction fees, their determinants, and their significance in the overall functioning of the Bitcoin network.

Bitcoin operates on a decentralized network where miners validate and include transactions in blocks. Miners are paid with newly minted bitcoins and a transaction fees as they dedicate computational power to solving complex mathematical puzzles. These transaction fees incentivize miners to prioritize certain transactions over others, ensuring that the network remains efficient and that transactions are confirmed promptly.

In the early years of Bitcoin, when the block reward (the newly minted bitcoins for each block) was high, transaction fees were relatively low or even negligible. However, as the block reward decreases over time due to Bitcoin's fixed supply schedule, transaction fees become more critical for miners' economic incentives.
Several factors influence the determination of Bitcoin's transaction fees, and users must consider these factors when sending Bitcoin transactions.

Network congestion significantly impacts transaction fees. During times of high transaction volume, such as periods of intense market activity or when many users send transactions simultaneously, the demand for block space increases. As a result, users may need to attach higher transaction fees to ensure their transactions are included in a block promptly.

Bitcoin has a limited block size, which defines the maximum amount of data that can be included in a single block. Transactions consist of data; the larger the transaction size (in bytes), the more block space it occupies. Miners prioritize transactions based on their fee per byte (fee rate), so larger transactions with higher fees per byte are more attractive to miners.

Bitcoin's transaction fees operate within a fee market, where users bid for block space by offering higher transaction fees. When network congestion is high, users willing to pay higher fees gain a competitive advantage, as miners want to maximize their earnings, they give priority to transactions with larger fees.

Users can choose between different levels of transaction urgency when sending Bitcoin. If a transaction is not time-sensitive, users may opt for lower fees to save on costs. Conversely, urgent or time-sensitive transactions require higher fees to ensure prompt confirmation.

Some wallets offer dynamic fee settings, allowing users to adjust the transaction fee according to their preferences. These settings can be manual or automated, and users can select to pay a higher or lower fee depending on the speed and urgency of their transactions.

Bitcoin's transaction fees are typically denominated in satoshis per byte (sat/byte). A satoshi, the smallest unit of Bitcoin, equivalent to one hundred millionth of a bitcoin, or 0.00000001 BTC. When sending a transaction, users specify the transaction fee they are willing to pay per byte of data in the transaction. Miners then prioritize transactions based on their fee rate, selecting those with higher fee rates to include in the next block.

Wallets often provide fee estimation algorithms that calculate the optimal fee depending on the current network conditions. These algorithms consider factors such as recent block times, transaction volume, and fee market dynamics to recommend an appropriate fee for timely confirmation.

Over time, the Bitcoin community has experienced debates and discussions surrounding the scalability of the network and the need for efficient fee market dynamics. The implementation of Segregated Witness (SegWit) in August 2017 was a significant milestone aimed at increasing the efficiency of block space usage.

SegWit restructures the transaction data, separating the signature data (witness data) from the transaction inputs, resulting in smaller transaction sizes. As a result, transactions that utilize SegWit witness data can fit more data within the limited block size, effectively increasing the throughput of the Bitcoin network.

Adoption of SegWit by wallets and users is essential to maximizing the benefits of its efficiency gains. Transactions utilizing SegWit benefit from lower fee rates due to their smaller sizes, providing users with a cost-effective option for sending Bitcoin.

As the adoption of cryptocurrencies grows, transaction fees will remain a critical aspect of the network's functioning. The interplay between supply and demand for block space will determine the level of transaction fees needed to ensure timely and efficient confirmation of transactions.

Technological advancements like the Lightning Network offer potential solutions to scalability challenges and reduce on-chain transaction fees. The Lightning Network enables off-chain, instant, low-cost transactions by creating user payment channels. Transactions within the Lightning Network occur outside the main blockchain, significantly reducing the load on the network and enabling faster, cheaper transactions.

Challenges and improvements in transaction scalability

As Bitcoin continues to gain popularity and recognition as a transformative digital currency, it faces several challenges that impact its ability to scale effectively. One of the most pressing challenges is transaction scalability—the ability to process many transactions quickly and cost-effectively. In this section, we explore the key challenges that Bitcoin encounters regarding transaction scalability and the various improvements and solutions that have been proposed to address these issues.

Bitcoin's blockchain operates on a decentralized network, with miners validating and recording each transaction in blocks. However, the design of Bitcoin's blockchain presents inherent limitations in terms of transaction processing speed and capacity, leading to several scalability challenges.

The limited block size is capped at 1 megabyte (MB). This means that each block can only accommodate a certain number of transactions, leading to a restricted throughput of about 7 transactions per second (TPS). As the number of users and transactions on the network grows, this limit significantly hinders scalability.

Another challenge is the block time, which is set at approximately 10 minutes. While this ensures sufficient time for network consensus and security, it also means that transactions may experience delays before being confirmed in a block. Longer block times can lead to slower transaction processing and potential congestion during times of high demand.

Transaction fees and priority represent another hurdle for scalability. As the demand for block space increases, users may need to offer higher transaction fees to incentivize miners to entail their transactions in the next block. This can result in escalating transaction fees during periods of network congestion, making Bitcoin less cost-effective for everyday transactions.

Additionally, some scalability proposals that involve increasing block sizes or modifying the network have raised concerns about potential centralization. Larger blocks could require more storage and computational resources, potentially favoring larger and more centralized mining operations.

To address the scalability challenges, the Bitcoin community has explored various improvements and solutions to enhance the network's transaction processing capabilities.

One notable improvement is Segregated Witness (SegWit), implemented in August 2017. Segregated Witness separates the signature (witness) data from transaction data, effectively reducing the size of transactions. By segregating this data, more transactions can be included in each block, thereby increasing the overall transaction throughput of the network.

Another significant development is the Lightning Network, a layer-two scaling solution that operates off-chain. The Lightning Network creates payment channels between users, allowing them to conduct multiple transactions without each one being recorded on the main blockchain. This approach reduces on-chain congestion and significantly improves transaction scalability.

In addition to SegWit and the Lightning Network, other proposed solutions are being considered. Schnorr signatures, for instance, are cryptographic signatures that enable multiple signatories to combine their signatures into a single signature. This feature reduces transaction data size, thereby increasing block capacity and improving overall scalability.

The introduction of sidechains and drivechains is another avenue of exploration. These proposed separate chains can be pegged to the Bitcoin blockchain, allowing for experimentation with new features and functionalities without altering the main network. This approach could alleviate the burden on the main chain while exploring innovative scaling solutions.

Layered scaling solutions like state channels and plasma are also being researched and developed. The objective of these solutions is to enable off-chain transactions while preserving the primary blockchain's security and integrity.

Addressing transaction scalability involves careful consideration of trade-offs and community consensus. Proposals for changes to the Bitcoin protocol must undergo rigorous scrutiny and debate to ensure that they align with the network's security, decentralization, and immutability principles.

Increasing the block size, for example, may provide short-term scalability gains but could also lead to centralization concerns and compromise the ability of regular users to run full nodes. As a result, the community has not reached a consensus on this approach, and alternative solutions like the Lightning Network have gained traction due to their focus on off-chain scaling.

The development and implementation of improvements like SegWit and the Lightning Network have already shown promising results in increasing transaction throughput and reducing fees.

Continued research and development will be essential to explore new ideas and innovative solutions to optimize the Bitcoin network's scalability. The ongoing commitment to preserving decentralization, security, and inclusivity while enhancing scalability will shape the future of Bitcoin as a robust and scalable digital currency.

CHAPTER VIII

Bitcoin's Role in Digital Payments

Advantages and limitations of using Bitcoin for payments

The first cryptocurrency, Bitcoin, has attracted a lot of interest as a possible substitute for conventional fiat money for making payments. Bitcoin is a decentralized digital money that is popular for peer-to-peer transactions because it has a number of benefits. However, it also faces limitations that hinder its widespread adoption as a mainstream payment method. In this section, we delve into the advantages and limitations of using Bitcoin for payments, exploring its transformative potential and the challenges it must overcome to become a widely accepted medium of exchange.

One of Bitcoin's core strengths lies in its decentralized nature. It operates on a distributed network, without the need for central authorities or intermediaries. This decentralized architecture guarantees that no single entity controls the currency, giving users more financial freedom and autonomy over their funds. Users can send and also receive payments directly without relying on banks or payment processors, making it especially appealing in regions with limited access to traditional financial services.

Another advantage of using Bitcoin is its global accessibility. Bitcoin operates on the internet, making it accessible to anyone with an internet connection. This global accessibility breaks down barriers of traditional cross-border payments, enabling seamless and faster transactions between individuals or businesses across different countries. Bitcoin's borderless nature makes it an attractive option for international remittances, where traditional methods are often costly and time-consuming.

Bitcoin transactions typically involve lower fees than traditional payment systems, especially for international transfers. Traditional financial institutions often charge significant fees for cross-border transactions due to currency conversion and intermediary charges. Bitcoin's peer-to-peer nature and absence of intermediaries reduce transaction costs, making it more cost-effective for small and large payments.

Additionally, Bitcoin transactions can be processed relatively quickly compared to traditional banking methods. While conventional bank transfers may take several business days, Bitcoin transactions can be confirmed within minutes, especially if users attach an appropriate transaction fee. This speed is particularly advantageous for time-sensitive transactions or when funds must be transferred urgently.

Bitcoin has the potential to bridge the gap of financial inclusion, providing individuals in underserved regions with access to a global financial system. People without access to conventional banking services can use Bitcoin wallets and participate in the digital economy, opening up new opportunities for economic empowerment.
Despite these advantages, Bitcoin also faces limitations that must be addressed for wider adoption. One of the

primary challenges of using Bitcoin for payments is its price volatility. Bitcoin's value can fluctuate significantly over short periods, making it difficult for merchants and consumers to predict its purchasing power accurately. The rapid price changes may result in price discrepancies between the time of payment initiation and confirmation, which can lead to issues with pricing goods and services.

Bitcoin's scalability remains a significant challenge, particularly when the network experiences high transaction volumes. The limited block size and block time can result in congestion and delays, causing slower transaction processing during peak periods. While scalability solutions like the Lightning Network have been proposed, their widespread adoption is still in progress.

For Bitcoin to be accepted as a standard form of payment, widespread user education and adoption are crucial. Many potential users may find the concept of cryptocurrencies complex and unfamiliar, leading to hesitancy in using Bitcoin for payments. Overcoming this barrier requires robust educational efforts and user-friendly interfaces to ensure seamless and secure transactions.

The regulatory landscape surrounding cryptocurrencies, including Bitcoin, varies widely across different jurisdictions. Uncertainty and changing regulations can challenge businesses and users seeking to adopt Bitcoin for payments. Regulatory clarity is essential to foster a conducive Bitcoin adoption and usage environment. While Bitcoin's underlying technology, blockchain, is considered secure, individual users must take responsibility for securing their private keys and wallets. Any loss or compromise of private keys can lead to the loss of funds, highlighting the importance of proper security measures and precautions for users.

Adoption by merchants and payment processors

Bitcoin, the pioneering cryptocurrency, has gained significant attention and popularity since its inception in 2009. As a decentralized digital currency, Bitcoin offers unique features that make it an appealing option for merchants and payment processors. In this section, we explore the factors influencing Bitcoin's adoption by merchants and payment processors, its advantages to businesses, and the challenges that need to be addressed for broader acceptance in the mainstream economy.

Bitcoin's decentralized nature is one of its core strengths. It operates on a distributed network, without the need for central authorities or intermediaries. This decentralized architecture guarantees that no single entity controls the currency, giving users more financial freedom and autonomy over their funds. For merchants and payment processors, this decentralization means they can accept Bitcoin without relying on traditional banking systems, reducing processing delays and fees associated with conventional payment methods.

Another significant advantage for merchants is the reduced risk of chargebacks. Bitcoin transactions are irreversible, meaning it cannot be reversed once a payment is confirmed. This feature significantly reduces the risk of chargebacks, a common issue merchants face in traditional payment systems face. Chargebacks can result in financial losses and administrative burdens for businesses, making Bitcoin's irreversibility an attractive feature.

For merchants operating in industries with time-sensitive transactions, such as e-commerce or digital services, faster payment processing is crucial. Bitcoin transactions can be confirmed relatively quickly, especially if users pay an appropriate fee. While traditional bank transfers may take several business days, Bitcoin transactions can be confirmed within minutes. This speed is particularly advantageous for merchants seeking to provide instant access to products or services to their customers.

Bitcoin's borderless nature allows businesses to reach customers worldwide without needing complex currency conversion or additional payment gateways. This global accessibility opens up new markets for merchants and fosters financial inclusivity, enabling transactions with individuals in underserved regions. For merchants targeting international customers, accepting Bitcoin can be a cost-effective way to process payments and reduce transaction costs.

Accepting Bitcoin can also offer merchants increased privacy. Bitcoin transactions do not require revealing personal or sensitive information during payment. This can be appealing to customers concerned about data breaches or identity theft. Bitcoin payments can enhance customer trust and confidence in a merchant's payment system by providing an additional layer of privacy.

Bitcoin's appeal to tech-savvy customers is another factor driving its adoption by merchants and payment processors. Embracing Bitcoin can attract customers seeking businesses supporting their preferred payment method. By accepting Bitcoin, merchants signal their forward-thinking approach and may attract a niche customer base that prefers cryptocurrency payments.

Despite the advantages, Bitcoin's adoption by merchants and payment processors is not without challenges and concerns. One of the primary challenges is Bitcoin's price volatility. In brief intervals, there can be substantial fluctuations in the value of Bitcoin, making it difficult for merchants to predict its purchasing power accurately. Rapid price changes may result in price discrepancies between the time of payment initiation and confirmation, which can lead to issues with pricing goods and services.

The regulatory landscape surrounding cryptocurrencies varies across different jurisdictions. Depending on the regulatory environment in their operating regions, merchants and payment processors may face legal and compliance challenges. Regulatory uncertainty can create hesitancy among merchants to adopt Bitcoin as a payment method.

Integrating Bitcoin payments into existing business systems and processes can be a technical challenge. Merchants may need to invest in suitable payment gateways, accounting systems, and security measures to facilitate seamless Bitcoin transactions. Additionally, ensuring proper security measures for Bitcoin wallets and private keys is critical to safeguarding funds from potential cyber threats.

Furthermore, despite growing popularity, Bitcoin adoption among consumers is not yet universal. Merchants accepting Bitcoin may encounter limited customer demand, especially in regions where cryptocurrency usage is less prevalent. Wider consumer adoption of Bitcoin will be essential to drive its acceptance by merchants and payment processors.

The role of Lightning Network in fast and low-cost transactions

The Lightning Network, a second-layer scaling solution for the Bitcoin blockchain, has emerged as a promising technology to address the scalability challenges faced by

Bitcoin. As the popularity of Bitcoin grew, so did the concern over its limited transaction throughput and increasing fees. The Lightning Network aims to enable fast and low-cost transactions, making Bitcoin more practical for everyday use. In this section, we explore the role of the Lightning Network in facilitating fast and low- cost transactions, its underlying technology, its advantages, and the challenges it faces in achieving widespread adoption.

Bitcoin's success as a decentralized digital currency also brought scalability challenges to the forefront. The original design of the Bitcoin blockchain allowed for a limited number of transactions to be processed within each block. As the number of users and transactions grew, the network's limited capacity became a bottleneck, leading to slower transaction processing times and higher fees during peak demand.

The slow and expensive transactions significantly hindered Bitcoin's use for everyday payments. For Bitcoin to become a practical medium of exchange, a scaling solution was needed to address these issues effectively. The Lightning Network emerged as a promising solution to unlock Bitcoin's full potential for fast and low-cost transactions.

The Lightning Network operates as a second-layer protocol on top of the Bitcoin blockchain. It leverages Bitcoin's underlying technology, the blockchain, while introducing off-chain payment channels to enable faster and cheaper transactions.

In the Lightning Network, two parties open a payment channel by creating a multi-signature transaction on the Bitcoin blockchain. This transaction serves as the opening of the channel, and the parties involved can now transact with each other off-chain. By conducting transactions off-chain, the Lightning Network reduces the burden on the main blockchain, easing congestion and speeding up transaction processing.

The off-chain nature of the Lightning Network allows for almost instantaneous transaction confirmations and dramatically reduces transaction fees. This is achieved by eliminating the need for each transaction to be individually confirmed and recorded on the main blockchain. Instead, transactions within the payment channel are only settled and recorded on the blockchain when the channel is closed, aggregating multiple transactions into a single on-chain transaction.

One of the most significant advantages of the Lightning Network is its ability to facilitate instant transactions. Since transactions occur off-chain within the payment channel, parties involved can transact with each other without waiting for block confirmations on the main blockchain. This near-instantaneous settlement is ideal for microtransactions and day-to-day payments.

By reducing the number of on-chain transactions, the Lightning Network significantly lowers transaction fees. Users only need to pay a small fee when opening and closing the payment channel, making frequent and small transactions more economically viable.

The Lightning Network effectively scales Bitcoin's transaction capacity by enabling a high volume of transactions to occur off-chain. As a result, the network can handle many microtransactions and everyday payments without congesting the main blockchain.

The Lightning Network provides users an additional layer of privacy by conducting transactions off-chain. Parties involved in a payment channel do not need to broadcast every transaction publicly, enhancing privacy and reducing the risk of information exposure.

Despite its potential, the Lightning Network faces several challenges and limitations that must be addressed for wider adoption.

The Lightning Network's success depends on liquidity availability within payment channels. For larger transactions to occur between parties that do not have a direct payment channel, liquidity routing must be established through interconnected payment channels. Ensuring sufficient liquidity and efficient routing remains a technical challenge.

As the Lightning Network relies on the underlying security of the Bitcoin blockchain, any vulnerabilities or attacks on the main blockchain could potentially affect Lightning Network transactions. Ensuring robust security measures is essential to maintain the integrity and trustworthiness of the Lightning Network.

The Lightning Network's user experience can be perceived as more complex than traditional payment methods. Users must be familiar with opening and closing payment channels, managing funds within channels, and monitoring transaction routing. Improving user-friendly interfaces and reducing technical barriers is crucial for widespread adoption.

While the Lightning Network aims to decentralize transactions, centralization concerns may arise in specific scenarios. Large payment processors or liquidity providers could control significant portions of the network, potentially leading to the centralization of payment channels.

CHAPTER IX

Bitcoin Regulation and Legal Considerations

Overview of global regulatory approaches

As Bitcoin and other cryptocurrencies gained popularity and recognition, governments and regulatory authorities worldwide have grappled with the challenge of developing appropriate frameworks to govern their use. The decentralized and borderless nature of cryptocurrencies like Bitcoin has presented unique regulatory complexities, with different countries adopting various approaches to address these emerging financial assets. In this section, we provide an overview of the global regulatory approaches on Bitcoin, exploring how different countries have responded to the rise of cryptocurrencies, the regulatory trends observed, and the challenges and opportunities that lie ahead.

One of the primary considerations in regulating Bitcoin is determining its legal status. Different countries have taken diverse approaches to acknowledge cryptocurrencies within their legal frameworks. Some have embraced Bitcoin as legal tender, recognizing it as a means of payment for goods and services. Some nations have allowed businesses to take Bitcoin in addition to conventional fiat currencies, such as El Salvador, which became the very first country to adopt Bitcoin as legal cash in 2021.

Conversely, some nations have taken a cautious approach, refraining from granting Bitcoin any legal tender status and treating it solely as a commodity or digital asset. This distinction can impact taxation, regulatory oversight, and the extent of consumer protections provided.

Several countries have established licensing and registration requirements for businesses engaged in cryptocurrency-related activities. Exchanges, wallet providers, and other cryptocurrency service providers may need to comply with specific regulatory obligations to operate legally within these jurisdictions. Licensing frameworks aim to protect consumers, mitigate money laundering risks, and foster a more transparent and accountable cryptocurrency ecosystem.

However, the implementation of licensing and registration requirements can vary significantly across countries. Some have embraced more stringent measures, while others have adopted a more lenient approach, allowing businesses to operate with minimal regulatory oversight.

Compliance with Combating the Financing of Terrorism (CFT) and Anti-Money Laundering (AML) regulations has been a top priority for regulators worldwide. Cryptocurrencies' pseudonymous nature has raised apprehensions about their potential misuse for illicit activities. Many countries have mandated cryptocurrency service providers to implement robust AML/CFT measures and report suspicious transactions to address these risks. A number of countries have matched their cryptocurrency laws to the guidelines provided by the Financial Action Task Force (FATF), an international organization that works to prevent money laundering and the funding of terrorism. Adherence to these international guidelines strengthens the cryptocurrency industry's integrity and helps establish a more credible and secure environment.

Taxation policies related to cryptocurrencies vary widely among countries. The treatment of Bitcoin for tax purposes can impact its attractiveness as an investment or payment option. Some countries view Bitcoin as property, subjecting it to capital gains tax when exchanged for fiat or other assets. Others consider it as a currency or commodity, imposing value-added tax (VAT) or goods and services tax (GST) on transactions involving Bitcoin.

The complexity of cryptocurrency taxation lies in determining the fair market value of cryptocurrencies at the time of the transaction, especially considering Bitcoin's price volatility. Clear and consistent tax guidelines are crucial for both individual investors and businesses to comply with their tax obligations.

Ensuring investor protection and consumer safeguards is a key objective for regulators when dealing with cryptocurrencies. Countries have introduced measures to prevent fraudulent Initial Coin Offerings (ICOs), Ponzi schemes, and other scams in the cryptocurrency space. Regulators have warned the public about the risks associated with investing in cryptocurrencies and have encouraged individuals to exercise caution and conduct thorough research before participating in the market.

Some countries have also introduced mechanisms to facilitate consumer complaints and dispute resolution related to cryptocurrency services. This enhances transparency and accountability within the industry and builds trust among consumers.

The borderless nature of cryptocurrencies raises challenges in enforcing regulatory measures across jurisdictions. Some countries have expressed concerns about cross-border transactions, money laundering, and tax evasion facilitated by cryptocurrencies. To address these concerns, international cooperation and information sharing among regulatory authorities have become increasingly important.

The G20, FATF, and other international organizations have facilitated discussions and collaboration among countries on cryptocurrency-related regulatory matters. Harmonizing regulatory approaches and fostering a unified global framework can help mitigate regulatory arbitrage and promote a more consistent and effective regulatory environment.

While regulatory approaches on Bitcoin vary, several common challenges and opportunities are evident. Lack of regulatory clarity remains a significant challenge for businesses and individuals in cryptocurrency. Ambiguous regulations can deter innovation and investment and may lead to businesses seeking more favorable regulatory environments in other countries.

The fast-paced and innovative nature of the cryptocurrency industry demands regulatory frameworks that strike a balance between fostering innovation and protecting consumers. Policymakers must stay abreast of technological advancements to ensure regulations remain relevant and effective.

Achieving global coordination and consensus on cryptocurrency regulations can be challenging, given the differing priorities and interests of countries. However, international cooperation is crucial to address cross-border issues and prevent regulatory arbitrage.

Given that they give underprivileged and unbanked people access to financial services, cryptocurrencies have the potential to improve financial inclusion. Regulators must balance risk mitigation and promoting financial inclusion through appropriate regulations.

Challenges in regulating a decentralized currency

The appearance of decentralized currencies, such as Bitcoin and other cryptocurrencies, has presented unique challenges for regulatory authorities worldwide. Unlike traditional fiat currencies, decentralized currencies operate without a central authority, making them difficult to control and monitor. In this section, we explore the challenges regulators face in establishing effective regulatory frameworks for decentralized currencies, the complexities of overseeing a global and borderless financial system, and the potential implications for the future of finance.

One of the primary challenges in regulating a decentralized currency lies in its very nature - the absence of a central authority. Traditional financial systems are built on centralized institutions like central banks and regulatory bodies that oversee and control money issuance, distribution, and management.

However, cryptocurrencies operate on a peer-to-peer network, eliminating the need for intermediaries. This lack of central authority makes it difficult for regulators to control the currency's supply, issuance, and distribution. Without a central entity to hold accountable, regulating decentralized currencies becomes complex, as traditional regulatory approaches may not be directly applicable.

Decentralized currencies are inherently borderless, allowing users to conduct transactions across international boundaries without intermediaries. While this feature enhances financial inclusivity and accessibility, it also poses challenges for regulators. Traditional financial regulations are typically limited to a specific jurisdiction, but decentralized currencies operate globally. Regulators must navigate the complexities of cross-border transactions, money laundering risks, and tax evasion, which can be challenging to monitor and address effectively without international cooperation and harmonized regulatory standards.

Cryptocurrencies provide a level of pseudonymity, allowing users to transact without revealing their real identities. While this feature offers privacy benefits, it also raises concerns about potential misuse for illicit activities, such as money laundering, terrorist financing, and other criminal endeavors. Balancing the need for privacy with the necessity to prevent financial crimes presents a challenge for regulators. Achieving the proper balance necessitates putting strong anti-money laundering (also known as AML) and combating the financing of terrorism (CFT) mechanisms in place without jeopardizing personal privacy.

The quick pace of technological advancements in the cryptocurrency space often outpaces regulatory developments. The decentralized nature of cryptocurrencies allows for continuous innovation and the emergence of new financial products and services. However, regulatory frameworks may take longer to adapt to these innovations, resulting in a regulatory lag. This lag can create uncertainties for businesses and consumers, hinder innovation, and potentially lead to a fragmented regulatory landscape across different jurisdictions.

Blockchain technology evolution has given rise to smart contracts and decentralized finance (DeFi) platforms. These systems operate autonomously based on predefined rules, and their complex nature poses challenges for regulatory oversight. Regulators must understand the intricacies of smart contracts and DeFi protocols to ensure they comply with existing laws and regulations, safeguard investor interests, and prevent potential risks associated with unregulated financial activities.

Protecting consumers is a fundamental aspect of financial regulation. However, cryptocurrency transactions' decentralized and often anonymous nature can make it challenging to hold bad actors accountable and provide adequate consumer protection. Cases of fraud, scams, and exchange hacks have highlighted the need for stronger consumer protection measures. Regulators face the challenge of balancing fostering innovation and ensuring consumer safety within a decentralized ecosystem.

Cryptocurrencies, especially those with smaller market capitalization, are susceptible to high volatility. Rapid price fluctuations can lead to significant investor risks and potential losses. Regulators must address the risks of investing in decentralized currencies while recognizing the unique characteristics that attract investors to this asset class. Educating investors about the inherent risks and fostering transparency in the cryptocurrency market are essential steps in mitigating these challenges.

As decentralized currencies operate globally, effective regulation requires international coordination and harmonization of standards. Inconsistent regulatory approaches across different jurisdictions can create regulatory arbitrage and hinder the development of a cohesive and well-regulated global financial system. Cooperation among countries is crucial in addressing cross-border challenges, establishing a level playing field for market participants, and preventing regulatory gaps that bad actors may exploit.

Future prospects for Bitcoin's legal status

As Bitcoin continues to gain popularity and recognition as a digital asset and means of financial exchange, its legal status remains a topic of significant interest and debate. Governments, financial institutions, and regulatory bodies worldwide are grappling with how to approach and regulate this revolutionary technology. In this section, we explore the future prospects for Bitcoin's legal status, examining the various approaches different countries take and the potential implications for the cryptocurrency's growth and integration into the global financial system.

The legal status of Bitcoin varies significantly from one country to another, as different jurisdictions grapple with the challenges as well as opportunities presented by digital currencies. Some nations have embraced Bitcoin and other cryptocurrencies, recognizing them as legitimate means of payment and investment. In contrast, others have expressed skepticism and imposed restrictive regulations to mitigate perceived risks, such as money laundering, fraud, and potential threats to financial stability.

Some countries have enacted regulatory frameworks that provide clarity and guidance for individuals and businesses engaging with Bitcoin. These regulations aim to balance fostering innovation and safeguarding consumers and investors. Such legal clarity encourages greater adoption of Bitcoin, as individuals and businesses feel more confident about participating in the cryptocurrency ecosystem.

Other countries have taken a cautious approach, adopting a wait-and-see stance to observe how the cryptocurrency landscape unfolds before crafting specific regulations. While this approach allows for a more flexible response to emerging trends, it can also lead to uncertainty and ambiguity for stakeholders operating in the cryptocurrency space.

On the international stage, Bitcoin's legal status faces unique challenges due to its borderless and decentralized nature. The lack of a centralized authority governing Bitcoin's issuance and operation makes it challenging to apply traditional legal frameworks. As a result, countries often face difficulties in enforcing regulatory compliance and addressing cross-border transactions involving cryptocurrencies.

Looking ahead, the future prospects for Bitcoin's legal status will likely be shaped by a combination of technological advancements, geopolitical factors, and evolving regulatory landscapes. One possible scenario is increased collaboration between governments and regulatory bodies at both national and international levels. Collaborative efforts could lead to establishing standardized guidelines for cryptocurrency regulation, promoting a more consistent and harmonized approach to the legal treatment of Bitcoin.

Furthermore, advancements in blockchain technology, privacy solutions, and user identification systems may address some of the concerns associated with cryptocurrency usage. For instance, developments in blockchain analytics tools could help governments and financial institutions track and monitor illicit activities, offering greater transparency and traceability within the cryptocurrency ecosystem.

The prospect of CBDCs (central bank digital currencies) also has implications for Bitcoin's legal status. Several central banks are actively exploring the development of CBDCs, representing digital versions of traditional fiat currencies issued and regulated by central authorities. The introduction of CBDCs could lead to increased competition between digital currencies, with potential implications for decentralized cryptocurrencies like Bitcoin's role and legal status.

As the global financial landscape evolves, the influence of major economies on Bitcoin's legal status cannot be overlooked. Decisions made by economic powerhouses, such as the United States, the European Union, and China, can significantly impact the regulatory environment for cryptocurrencies worldwide. Balancing fostering innovation and protecting financial stability remains a delicate and complex task, and these economic giants will likely influence the legal treatment of Bitcoin.

The legal status of Bitcoin also intertwines with discussions about financial inclusion. In regions where conventional banking infrastructure is limited, Bitcoin and other cryptocurrencies offer a potential solution to enhance financial access and inclusion. Regulators must carefully consider how to address cryptocurrencies' unique challenges and opportunities to promote financial inclusion while mitigating risks.

Moreover, the ongoing efforts to address environmental concerns related to Bitcoin mining may affect its legal status. As sustainability becomes a global priority, regulators may look to encourage energy-efficient mining practices or explore alternative consensus mechanisms to reduce Bitcoin's carbon footprint.

CHAPTER X

Bitcoin and Financial Inclusion

Bitcoin's potential impact on the unbanked and underbanked

Access to essential financial services, including bank accounts and credit, is fundamental to economic development and financial inclusion. However, a major portion of the global population remains unbanked or underbanked, lacking access to traditional financial systems. In recent years, Bitcoin, the pioneering cryptocurrency, has emerged as a potential tool for empowering the unbanked and underbanked populations. In this section, we explore Bitcoin's potential impact on the unbanked and underbanked, examining its advantages, challenges, and broader implications for financial inclusion.

One of the primary benefits of Bitcoin for the unbanked and underbanked is accessibility. Unlike traditional banking services that require physical infrastructure, Bitcoin can be accessed using a smartphone and an internet connection. This digital accessibility lowers barriers to entry for individuals in remote or underserved regions, enabling them to participate in the global economy.

Cross-border remittances are vital in the economies of many developing nations, with millions of people relying on money sent by family members working abroad.

However, traditional remittance services often come with high fees and delays. Bitcoin's borderless nature allows for fast and low-cost cross-border transactions, potentially reducing remittance costs and enabling more efficient money transfers.

In regions with unstable economies or high inflation rates, the unbanked and underbanked often face challenges in preserving the value of their money. Bitcoin's decentralized and fixed supply nature provides an alternative store of value that is not subject to the monetary policies of any central authority. Individuals can have more control over their financial assets, protecting them from currency devaluation and economic instability.

As the global economy increasingly shifts towards digital transactions, the unbanked and underbanked risk being further excluded from economic opportunities. Bitcoin's digital nature enables these populations to participate in the digital economy, opening up possibilities for e-commerce, online work opportunities, and access to a broader range of financial products and services.

While Bitcoin presents promising opportunities for the unbanked and underbanked, several challenges and barriers must be addressed. Firstly, there is the issue of digital literacy. Many unbanked individuals may lack the necessary knowledge and skills to use cryptocurrencies effectively and securely. Educational initiatives and user-friendly tools are crucial in bridging this knowledge gap.

Bitcoin's inherent price volatility can be a concern for the unbanked and underbanked, who may not be familiar with the risks associated with holding and transacting in cryptocurrencies. Price fluctuations can lead to potential losses or increased financial risks, especially for those who rely on Bitcoin as a store of value or means of remittance.

While Bitcoin's digital accessibility is a significant advantage, access to smartphones and reliable internet connectivity can still be limited in some regions. The lack of necessary infrastructure may hinder widespread adoption among the unbanked and underbanked.

Regulatory frameworks for cryptocurrencies vary widely across different countries. Uncertainty around regulatory policies may create barriers to entry for service providers looking to offer Bitcoin-related financial services to the unbanked and underbanked. Clear and supportive regulations can foster an environment conducive to financial inclusion through Bitcoin.

Promoting financial inclusion through Bitcoin requires a concerted effort to educate the unbanked and underbanked about the risks, benefits, and responsible use of cryptocurrencies. Financial literacy programs can empower individuals to make knowledgeable decisions and maximize the benefits of using Bitcoin for their financial needs.

Cross-border remittances and reduced fees

Cross-border remittances, the transfer of money from one country to another, are vital in supporting families and economies worldwide. However, traditional remittance systems often come with high fees, long processing times, and limited accessibility, especially for individuals in underserved regions. In recent years, Bitcoin, the pioneering cryptocurrency, has emerged as a potential solution for cross-border remittances, offering the promise of reduced fees, faster transactions, and enhanced financial inclusion. In this section, we explore Bitcoin's role in cross-border remittances and its potential to revolutionize the remittance industry, examining its advantages, challenges, and the broader implications for global financial systems.

One of the main benefits of employing Bitcoin for cross-border remittances is its borderless nature. Traditional remittance systems often involve multiple intermediaries, such as banks and payment processors, leading to higher fees and longer processing times. With Bitcoin, cross-border transactions occur directly on its decentralized network, bypassing intermediaries and reducing costs. This direct peer-to-peer nature of Bitcoin transfers allows for faster and more efficient remittances, especially for individuals sending money to countries with limited banking infrastructure.

Bitcoin's lower transaction fees than traditional remittance services are a significant draw for many users. Traditional remittance providers often charge a percentage of the transfer amount, which can be particularly burdensome for small remittances. In contrast, Bitcoin transaction fees are typically much lower, making it an attractive option for transferring smaller amounts of money across borders. This cost-effectiveness enhances the value of remittances received by recipients, enabling them to make more meaningful use of the funds.

Cross-border remittances using traditional banking systems can take several days or even longer to reach the recipient's account. This delay can be especially challenging for families relying on remittances for immediate financial needs. On the other hand, Bitcoin transactions can be completed within minutes, significantly reducing the time it takes for funds to be available to the recipient. This speed and efficiency make Bitcoin appealing for those seeking faster cross-border transfers.

Traditional remittance services may have limited reach in certain regions, leaving many individuals without access to reliable and affordable cross-border transfer options. Bitcoin's accessibility requires only an internet connection and a digital wallet, enabling individuals in remote or underserved areas to participate in cross-border remittances. This broader access to remittance services can increase financial inclusion and empower individuals lacking viable options for sending and receiving money internationally.

While Bitcoin offers promising advantages for cross-border remittances, it also faces several challenges and risks that must be addressed. One of the primary concerns is price volatility. Bitcoin's value can fluctuate significantly over short periods, exposing senders and recipients to potential gains or losses. Such volatility can introduce uncertainty in remittance amounts, impacting the stability of recipients' financial resources.

The regulatory landscape for cryptocurrencies, including Bitcoin, varies widely across different countries. As governments and financial regulators grapple with classifying and overseeing cryptocurrencies, potential regulation changes may impact Bitcoin's role in cross-border remittances. Uncertainty in the regulatory environment can generate challenges for service providers and users seeking consistent and compliant remittance solutions.

For Bitcoin to realize its full potential in cross-border remittances, broader adoption and increased education are essential. Both senders and recipients must understand the benefits and risks of using Bitcoin for remittances. Additionally, service providers must create user-friendly and accessible platforms that encourage adoption while addressing concerns related to security and privacy.

The network's scalability and transaction throughput become crucial as Bitcoin's popularity grows. Scaling challenges could lead to network congestion and longer confirmation times, potentially hampering the efficiency and appeal of Bitcoin for cross-border remittances. Scalability solutions, such as the Lightning Network, are being developed to address these issues and improve the network's capacity for handling higher transaction volumes.

Bitcoin operates independently of traditional currencies, and exchange rates between Bitcoin and fiat currencies can fluctuate. This exchange rate risk adds another layer of complexity to cross-border remittances involving Bitcoin. Users must consider currency conversion rates and fees when sending and receiving funds, as they may impact remittances' overall cost and value.

Trust and security are crucial factors in cross-border remittances, where individuals rely on timely and secure delivery of funds. While Bitcoin's underlying technology, blockchain, provides robust security measures, users must exercise caution and adopt best practices to protect their digital wallets and prevent fraud or hacking attempts.

Case studies of Bitcoin adoption in developing countries

Bitcoin, the pioneering cryptocurrency, has garnered attention worldwide for its ability to disrupt traditional financial systems and offer financial inclusion to underserved populations. While Bitcoin adoption has been prominent in developed countries, its impact in developing nations is equally noteworthy. In this section, we explore case studies of Bitcoin adoption in developing countries, examining the factors driving adoption, the challenges faced, and the transformative potential of decentralized digital currencies in improving financial access and empowering communities.

Venezuela, a country plagued by hyperinflation and economic instability, provides a compelling case study for Bitcoin adoption. The nation's currency, the bolívar, has experienced astronomical inflation rates, leading to a loss of value and erosion of purchasing power for its citizens. In response to this economic crisis, many Venezuelans turned to Bitcoin as a store of value and a means of preserving their wealth. With access to the internet and smartphones becoming more widespread, Bitcoin offered an alternative currency that could shield individuals from the rapid devaluation of the bolívar. Despite regulatory challenges and occasional crackdowns on cryptocurrency use, Bitcoin has gained popularity as a financial survival and empowerment tool in Venezuela.

Nigeria, Africa's largest economy, has witnessed a significant rise in Bitcoin adoption, driven by its youthful and tech-savvy population. The country faces challenges in accessing traditional financial services, especially in rural areas. Bitcoin's digital accessibility has appealed to many Nigerians, allowing them to partake in the global economy and engage in cross-border transactions. Additionally, Bitcoin's potential for remittances has been instrumental for Nigerian families receiving money from relatives abroad. Its lower fees and faster transaction times than traditional remittance services have provided a more efficient means of receiving funds, supporting economic activities and livelihoods.

Kenya, known for its innovative mobile money ecosystem, provides an interesting backdrop for Bitcoin adoption. While mobile money services like M-Pesa have successfully brought financial services to the unbanked, Bitcoin has emerged as an alternative digital payment method. Kenyan entrepreneurs and freelancers have embraced Bitcoin to receive payments for their services globally. Its borderless nature and lower transaction fees offer advantages for cross-border transactions, supporting Kenya's burgeoning digital economy. However, regulatory uncertainties and concerns over scams have also been present, requiring greater education and awareness to ensure responsible Bitcoin usage.

Argentina, like Venezuela, has faced economic turmoil and currency devaluation. In the face of financial instability, Argentinians have sought refuge in Bitcoin as a hedge against inflation. Many individuals view Bitcoin as a more stable store of value, preserving their wealth amid the country's economic uncertainties. Furthermore, Argentinians seeking access to international markets and opportunities have embraced Bitcoin's potential for cross-border transactions. The country's tech-savvy population has driven grassroots adoption and fostered a growing Bitcoin community, despite regulatory challenges and varying degrees of acceptance from financial institutions.

In the Philippines, Bitcoin has gained traction as a means of financial inclusion and remittance facilitation. The country has a significant portion of its population working abroad, and remittances are crucial in supporting families back home. Bitcoin's lower fees and faster transaction times have become an attractive option for cross-border remittances, providing recipients with more substantial funds and reducing the reliance on traditional remittance services. Moreover, Bitcoin has found use in supporting local businesses and e-commerce, contributing to the country's digital economy.

While Bitcoin adoption in developing countries presents numerous opportunities, it also faces several challenges. Price volatility, regulatory uncertainty, lack of infrastructure, and concerns over scams and security are some of the barriers to adoption. Addressing these challenges requires governments, financial institutions, and cryptocurrency community collaborative efforts.

The case studies of Bitcoin adoption in developing countries demonstrate several key benefits. Financial inclusion, access to global markets, reduced remittance costs, and enhanced financial sovereignty are among the advantages observed in these communities. Bitcoin has the ability to empower individuals and support economic growth in regions where traditional financial systems have limitations.

The transformative potential of Bitcoin adoption in developing countries lies in its ability to democratize finance and provide opportunities for economic upliftment. By leveraging blockchain technology and decentralized networks, Bitcoin can create more inclusive financial systems and reduce the dependency on traditional banking intermediaries. Furthermore, Bitcoin's potential as a secure and transparent payment method can foster trust and financial stability in regions grappling with economic challenges.

The case studies of Bitcoin adoption in developing countries underscore the transformative potential of decentralized digital currencies in improving financial access and empowering communities. Venezuela, Nigeria, Kenya, Argentina, and the Philippines are among the nations where Bitcoin has found adoption and offered unique advantages in the face of economic uncertainties and limited financial services. However, price volatility, regulatory uncertainty, infrastructure, and education challenges remain prevalent.

For Bitcoin adoption to reach its full potential in developing countries, supportive regulatory frameworks, financial literacy programs, and robust infrastructure are essential. By fostering an enabling environment for digital currencies, governments and financial institutions can harness the power of Bitcoin to drive financial inclusion, support economic growth, and empower individuals in underserved regions. As the world embraces digital finance, Bitcoin's role in developing countries promises to create a more inclusive and sustainable future for global financial systems.

CHAPTER XI

Bitcoin's Impact on Investments and the Economy

Bitcoin as a store of value and investment asset

The pioneering cryptocurrency, Bitcoin, has shown to be a useful asset that can be used as an investment vehicle as well as a store of value. Since its launch in 2009, Bitcoin has developed from a modern virtual currency to a reputable store of value that draws in institutions and investors from all over the world. In this section, we explore the dual role of Bitcoin as a store of value and investment asset, examining its characteristics, historical performance, advantages, risks, and broader implications for the financial landscape.

A store of value is an asset that retains its purchasing power over time, preserving wealth and protecting against inflation. Traditionally, valuable metals such as gold and silver have served as stores of value. However, Bitcoin's emergence as a digital store of value marks a significant shift in the financial landscape. Bitcoin's fixed supply, scarcity, and decentralized nature make it appealing to individuals seeking an alternative to traditional fiat currencies susceptible to central bank interventions and inflationary pressures. As a digital asset, Bitcoin can be stored securely in digital wallets, offering a more convenient and accessible store of value for the digital age.

Bitcoin's journey as a store of value has been marked by extraordinary price appreciation and volatility. Over the years, it has experienced significant price fluctuations, leading to polarized opinions regarding its suitability as a store of value. Advocates point to Bitcoin's impressive long-term returns, highlighting its potential to outpace traditional assets like stocks and bonds. On the other hand, detractors raise concerns about price volatility, arguing that it may hinder its stability as a reliable store of value.

Bitcoin offers several advantages as a store of value. Its decentralized nature ensures that it is not subject to the control of any central authority, reducing the risk of currency devaluation or government intervention. Additionally, Bitcoin's fixed supply of 21 million coins creates a deflationary effect, potentially leading to increased value over time as demand outstrips supply. As a digital asset, Bitcoin provides ease of storage and transfer, enabling individuals to retain control of their wealth without relying on intermediaries.

While Bitcoin holds promise as a store of value, it also faces risks and considerations. Price volatility remains a significant concern, as it may deter risk-averse individuals from considering Bitcoin as a reliable store of wealth. Regulatory uncertainty in some jurisdictions could impact its long-term viability as a store of value, and security risks related to potential hacking or digital wallet vulnerabilities must be carefully managed. As with any investment, diversification and risk management strategies are crucial for those considering Bitcoin as a store of value.

In addition to its role as a store of value, Bitcoin has increasingly gained traction as an investment asset. Institutional and retail investors have turned to Bitcoin as a means of portfolio diversification and potential higher returns. As the first and most well-known cryptocurrency, Bitcoin has enjoyed a significant "first-mover advantage," drawing attention and investments from various stakeholders in the financial markets.

Bitcoin's investment performance has been nothing short of remarkable. Bitcoin's price surged from mere cents to several dollars in its early years, attracting early adopters and technology enthusiasts. The 2017 bull run saw Bitcoin's price reach an all-time high of nearly $20,000, further cementing its status as a lucrative investment opportunity. While the subsequent market correction led to price retracement, Bitcoin's ability to rebound and continue attracting investor interest underscores its resilience and potential as an investment asset.

As an investment asset, Bitcoin offers unique advantages. Its potential for high returns has been a driving force behind its growing popularity. Some investors view Bitcoin as a hedge against economic uncertainties and inflation, similar to gold and other traditional safe-haven assets. Additionally, Bitcoin's liquidity and accessibility on various cryptocurrency exchanges make it easier for investors to buy and sell, further contributing to its attractiveness as an investment vehicle.

Investing in Bitcoin carries inherent risks that investors must carefully consider. Price volatility remains a primary concern, with sharp price swings impacting short-term investment strategies. Lack of regulation and potential regulatory changes in cryptocurrency can also create uncertainty for investors. Moreover, Bitcoin's absence of intrinsic value leaves it susceptible to speculative market behaviors and price manipulation, which may challenge its long-term investment viability.

Bitcoin's dual role as a store of value and an investment asset has broader implications for the financial landscape. As an alternative store of value, Bitcoin challenges the traditional concept of money and the role of central banks in currency management. As an investment asset, Bitcoin's rise has sparked interest in the broader cryptocurrency market, leading to the development of novel financial products and investment opportunities.

Market trends and fluctuations in Bitcoin's price

Bitcoin, the pioneering cryptocurrency, has experienced dramatic price fluctuations since its inception in 2009. As the first decentralized virtual currency, Bitcoin has captured the attention of investors, traders, as well as the broader financial community. In this section, we explore the market trends and fluctuations in Bitcoin's price, analyzing the factors driving its volatility, the historical price patterns, and the ramifications of these trends on the cryptocurrency market.

One of the defining features of Bitcoin is its extreme price volatility. Over the years, Bitcoin's price has seen significant ups and downs, often experiencing rapid and substantial price swings within short time frames. The price volatility of Bitcoin has been a subject of debate among investors and financial experts, with some viewing it as an opportunity for significant gains, while others consider it a potential risk that hinders its broader adoption as a stable means of exchange.

Several factors contribute to Bitcoin's price fluctuations. Market demand and supply dynamics play a crucial role, as increasing demand drives prices higher, while selling pressure leads to price declines. Additionally, news events, regulatory announcements, technological advancements, and macroeconomic trends can influence investor sentiment and impact Bitcoin's price movements. The scarcity of Bitcoin, with a fixed supply of 21 million coins, can also amplify price movements, as supply constraints contribute to higher price volatility.

A study of Bitcoin's historical price patterns reveals several recurring trends. Bitcoin has undergone multiple bull and bear cycles, characterized by periods of rapid price growth followed by sharp corrections. The 2017 bull run saw Bitcoin's price surge to an all-time high of nearly $20,000, only to experience a significant correction in the subsequent bear market. The 2020-2021 bull market witnessed another explosive price rally, driving Bitcoin's price above $60,000, but again followed by a notable correction. These cycles indicate the cyclical nature of Bitcoin's price movements, with periods of optimism and vitality often giving way to market corrections and consolidation.

Investor sentiment plays a crucial role in driving Bitcoin's price fluctuations. Positive news, endorsements from prominent figures, and institutional adoption can boost investor confidence and increase buying activity, driving higher prices. Conversely, negative news, regulatory concerns, or security incidents can trigger fear and uncertainty, leading to sell-offs and price declines. The interconnectedness of the cryptocurrency market means that events in one part of the world can have ripple effects on Bitcoin's price globally.

Speculation is another significant factor influencing Bitcoin's price volatility. Given its relative novelty and limited history, Bitcoin remains a speculative asset for many investors. Speculative trading, driven by short-term price movements, can amplify price fluctuations and create additional volatility in the market. While speculation can lead to substantial gains for some traders, it also carries risks, as rapid price swings can result in significant losses for others.

Bitcoin's price trends and fluctuations have broader implications for the entire cryptocurrency market. As the leading cryptocurrency, Bitcoin often sets the tone for market sentiment. Bull runs in Bitcoin often coincide with increased interest and investment in other cryptocurrencies, leading to what is commonly known as the "altseason," where alternative cryptocurrencies experience significant price surges. Conversely, bear markets in Bitcoin can lead to market-wide corrections and increased risk aversion among investors.

Given Bitcoin's price volatility, risk management is essential for investors and traders. Long-term investors may adopt a "buy and hold" strategy, believing in the long-term potential of Bitcoin and the cryptocurrency market. On the other hand, traders may utilize technical analysis and market indicators to identify short-term price trends and execute strategic trades. Proper risk diversification, setting stop-loss levels, and disciplined portfolio management are crucial for navigating the volatile cryptocurrency market.

The entry of institutional investors and large corporations into the cryptocurrency market has notably impacted Bitcoin's price trends. Institutional adoption has brought increased legitimacy and liquidity to the market, reducing some of the inherent volatility associated with early-stage markets. Moreover, the growing interest from institutional investors has signaled broader acceptance of Bitcoin as a legitimate asset class and a potential store of value.

As the cryptocurrency market continues to mature, Bitcoin's price fluctuations are expected to gradually stabilize. Increased regulatory clarity, growing adoption, and advancements in the underlying technology may contribute to reducing price volatility over time. However, given the nascent nature of the market and the evolving regulatory landscape, uncertainties and fluctuations are likely to persist in the near term.

The macroeconomic implications of widespread adoption

Bitcoin, the pioneering cryptocurrency, has garnered significant attention and interest since its introduction in 2009. As its adoption grows, discussions about the potential macroeconomic implications of widespread Bitcoin usage have become increasingly pertinent. This section explores the macroeconomic consequences of widespread Bitcoin adoption, analyzing its impact on traditional financial systems, monetary policies, international trade, financial inclusion, and government regulations.

The widespread adoption of Bitcoin could disrupt traditional financial systems, challenging the role of central banks and conventional financial institutions. As a decentralized digital currency, Bitcoin operates outside the purview of traditional financial intermediaries, offering individuals greater financial autonomy. The ease of cross-border transactions and low transaction fees associated with Bitcoin may reduce reliance on traditional banking channels, potentially reshaping the global financial landscape.

The widespread use of Bitcoin may influence how central banks formulate monetary policies. Traditional monetary policies involve adjusting interest rates and money supply to manage inflation and economic growth. With Bitcoin's fixed supply of 21 million coins, it cannot be subject to monetary expansion or deflationary measures, potentially challenging conventional inflation control methods. Policymakers may need to adapt their strategies to account for the presence of a non-governmental, deflationary digital currency.

Bitcoin's use in international trade has gained momentum in recent years. It offers advantages such as faster and cheaper cross-border transactions, making it an attractive substitute to traditional payment systems. If widely adopted, Bitcoin could challenge the dominance of conventional reserve currencies such as the US dollar and influence the dynamics of international trade. Countries may increasingly use Bitcoin for settlements, impacting exchange rate dynamics and altering global currency hierarchies.

In regions with insufficient access to traditional banking services, Bitcoin could facilitate financial inclusion. Individuals can create Bitcoin wallets and participate in the global financial ecosystem with a simple internet connection. Moreover, Bitcoin's decentralized nature enables individuals to bypass intermediaries, potentially lowering remittance transaction costs and facilitating financial transactions for the unbanked and underbanked populations.

Widespread Bitcoin adoption may prompt governments to develop regulatory frameworks to tackle the challenges and opportunities presented by cryptocurrencies. The lack of uniform regulations across jurisdictions poses a challenge, leading to potential regulatory arbitrage. Governments may seek to strike a balance between fostering innovation and safeguarding financial stability and consumer protection.

The increased adoption of Bitcoin introduces new risks to the broader financial system. Price volatility and speculative trading behavior may amplify systemic risks, particularly if many financial assets shift into cryptocurrencies. Additionally, potential disruptions in traditional financial systems due to technological glitches or cyberattacks on cryptocurrency exchanges may have far-reaching implications for economic stability.

The rise of Bitcoin has prompted some central banks to explore the idea of Central Bank Digital Currencies (CBDCs). CBDCs are virtual versions of fiat currencies issued and regulated by central banks. The widespread adoption of Bitcoin could expedite the development and implementation of CBDCs as central banks seek to maintain control over monetary systems and payment infrastructures.

As Bitcoin becomes more integrated into the global financial system, it may influence portfolio diversification strategies. Institutional investors and fund managers may allocate a portion of their portfolios to Bitcoin as a hedge against traditional asset classes. This integration could create a more interconnected and correlated global financial market.

Bitcoin's energy-intensive mining process has raised concerns about its environmental impact. Increased emphasis on energy-efficient consensus processes and a push for more environmentally friendly energy sources for mining operations could result from widespread adoption exacerbating these worries.

CHAPTER XII

Criticisms and Controversies Surrounding Bitcoin

Environmental concerns

Bitcoin, the pioneering cryptocurrency, has gained widespread attention for its potential to revolutionize the financial landscape. However, the effect of Bitcoin mining on the environment and energy consumption has become increasingly concerning. In this section, we delve into the environmental implications of Bitcoin, analyzing the energy-intensive mining process, the carbon footprint associated with Bitcoin transactions, and the ongoing efforts to address these concerns.

Bitcoin mining is a crucial process that validates transactions and places new blocks to the blockchain. Miners tackle challenging mathematical challenges with the help of powerful computers; the first miner to finish the puzzle wins freshly created Bitcoins. However, this mining process requires enormous computational power, leading to significant energy consumption. As the difficulty of mining increases with the growth of the Bitcoin network, the energy requirements continue to escalate.

The energy-intensive mining process directly contributes to Bitcoin's carbon footprint. The majority of mining operations depend on fossil fuels as their primary energy source, leading to a substantial emission of greenhouse gases into the atmosphere. Concerns over Bitcoin mining's effect on global carbon emissions and climate change are raised by the fact that its carbon footprint is similar to that of several small nations.

Bitcoin mining operations are often clustered in regions with abundant and relatively cheap energy, such as China and some parts of the United States. The concentration of mining activities in specific areas can strain local energy grids and natural resources. In some cases, mining activities have led to increased electricity demand and competition with residential and industrial users, affecting the overall sustainability of energy resources.

The rapid evolution of mining hardware has led to frequent upgrades and replacements, resulting in substantial electronic waste (e-waste). Outdated mining equipment is often discarded, contributing to the growing e-waste problem. Proper e-waste management and recycling practices are crucial to mitigate the environmental impact of mining hardware.

Recognizing the environmental concerns of Bitcoin, the cryptocurrency community and industry stakeholders have initiated various efforts to address these issues. Some miners are exploring using renewable energy sources, like the hydro, solar, and wind power, to reduce the carbon footprint of mining operations. Renewable energy solutions decrease the environmental impact and contribute to the decentralization of mining activities.

The energy-intensive proof-of-work (PoW) consensus mechanism, which underpins Bitcoin's security, has been the primary driver of its environmental concerns. In response to these challenges, developers are exploring alternative consensus mechanisms, such as proof-of-stake (PoS), requiring significantly less energy. PoS does not rely on mining, and instead, validators are selected based on the amount of coins they have and are willing to "stake" as collateral. This transition could dramatically reduce the environmental impact of cryptocurrency networks.

Layer 2 solutions, like Lightning Network for Bitcoin, offer scalability and faster transaction times while reducing the load on the main blockchain. By periodically processing many smaller transactions off-chain and settling them on the main blockchain, Layer 2 solutions can significantly decrease the energy consumption per transaction. Raising awareness about the environmental concerns of Bitcoin is crucial in encouraging responsible mining practices and energy consumption. Education and transparency within the cryptocurrency community can foster discussions on sustainability and drive positive change.

Collaboration with environmental organizations and researchers can provide valuable insights and expertise in addressing the environmental impact of Bitcoin. Initiatives that promote sustainable mining practices and carbon offset programs can help mitigate the adverse effects on the environment.

Volatility and market manipulation

Bitcoin, the pioneering cryptocurrency, has experienced significant price volatility since its inception. This volatility has been a subject of fascination and concern among investors and regulators. This section explores the factors contributing to Bitcoin's price volatility and the possibility for market manipulation within the cryptocurrency ecosystem.

Several factors contribute to the inherent volatility of Bitcoin's price. As a relatively new and evolving asset class, Bitcoin lacks a well-established valuation model, leading to speculative trading behavior. Additionally, its limited supply and increasing demand can result in sharp price fluctuations. News events, regulatory developments, macroeconomic factors, and technological advancements can also trigger rapid price movements.

The speculative nature of Bitcoin attracts both seasoned traders and retail investors seeking to capitalize on price fluctuations. The herd mentality often dominates the market sentiment, leading to extreme price swings driven by emotional reactions rather than fundamental analysis.

Bitcoin's market is relatively small compared to traditional financial markets. As a result, even moderate buy or sell orders can significantly impact the price due to low liquidity and shallow market depth.

Media coverage and social media platforms can amplify price movements by disseminating information and opinions to a vast audience. Positive or negative news can trigger a buying or selling frenzy, adding to Bitcoin's price volatility.

Market manipulation is a concerning issue within the cryptocurrency ecosystem. Various forms of manipulation, such as pump-and-dump schemes, wash trading, and spoofing, have been observed in Bitcoin markets. These practices distort the true market value of Bitcoin, leading to deceptive price movements and potential losses for unsuspecting traders.

The decentralized as well as global nature of the cryptocurrency market makes it difficult to regulate and monitor effectively. The absence of robust oversight and the presence of unregulated exchanges create an environment conducive to market manipulation.

The extreme volatility and potential for market manipulation in Bitcoin can erode investor confidence. Uncertainty about market integrity and the fear of significant losses can deter institutional investors from entering cryptocurrency.

Efforts to mitigate Bitcoin's price volatility and curb market manipulation are essential for the long-term stability and growth of the cryptocurrency market. Several measures can be considered:

Cryptocurrency exchanges should implement robust market surveillance mechanisms to detect and prevent suspicious trading activities. Collaboration with regulatory authorities can also aid in monitoring and curbing market manipulation.

Cryptocurrency exchanges should be encouraged to provide transparent and timely reporting of trading volumes, order books, and other relevant data. Greater transparency fosters investor trust and contributes to a more informed trading environment.

Educating investors about the risks associated with cryptocurrency trading and the potential for market manipulation is crucial. Enhancing financial literacy can empower investors to make knowledgeable decisions and protect themselves from fraudulent schemes.

Introducing well-defined regulatory frameworks for cryptocurrency markets can help deter market manipulation and ensure fair trading practices. Collaboration between industry stakeholders, governments, and regulators is necessary to balance innovation and investor protection.

The introduction of stablecoins and cryptocurrency derivatives may provide a degree of stability to the market. Stablecoins pegged to fiat currencies can act as a hedge against price volatility, while derivatives can enable risk management strategies for traders.

As Bitcoin and other cryptocurrencies find more significant real-world adoption and utility, their intrinsic value may become less influenced by speculative trading. Real-world use cases can help stabilize prices and reduce the impact of market sentiment on asset valuations.

Addressing misconceptions and debunking myths

Bitcoin, the pioneering cryptocurrency, has captured the imagination of people worldwide, sparking both enthusiasm and skepticism. However, misconceptions and myths surrounding Bitcoin have increased, leading to misunderstandings and misinformation. In this section, we aim to address some common misconceptions and debunk prevalent myths about Bitcoin, shedding light on its true nature and potential.

One of the most persistent myths about Bitcoin is that it offers complete anonymity, making it the preferred currency for illegal activities. In reality, Bitcoin is pseudonymous, not anonymous. Each transaction is recorded on the public blockchain, accessible to anyone. While users' identities are not explicitly tied to their wallets, transactions can be traced through blockchain analysis. Law enforcement agencies and regulatory bodies have established sophisticated tools to track illicit activities involving Bitcoin, making it a less attractive choice for criminals than commonly believed.

Detractors often label Bitcoin as a speculative bubble destined to burst, drawing parallels to historical market bubbles. While Bitcoin's price has experienced significant volatility, attributing its value solely to speculation overlooks its underlying technological and economic fundamentals. Bitcoin's finite supply, decentralized nature, and potential as a store of value contribute to its appeal among investors. While price corrections have occurred in the past, Bitcoin's resilience and continued adoption suggest that it is more than just a fleeting bubble.

Critics frequently argue that Bitcoin lacks intrinsic value because any tangible asset or government authority does not back it. However, Bitcoin's value derives from its trust and utility as a decentralized digital currency. Its scarcity, divisibility, portability, and the underlying blockchain technology contribute to its perceived value. Like any form of money, Bitcoin's value is ultimately determined by the trust and confidence of its users.

Another misconception is that Bitcoin is exclusively for tech-savvy individuals. While it is true that understanding the technical intricacies of blockchain technology can be beneficial, the user experience of Bitcoin has significantly improved over the years. Wallets and exchanges have become more user-friendly, allowing individuals with basic computer skills to acquire, store, and use Bitcoin easily.

A few high-profile cases have perpetuated the misconception that Bitcoin enables tax evasion. In reality, tax authorities have become increasingly adept at monitoring cryptocurrency transactions. Many countries have introduced clear guidelines on reporting and taxing cryptocurrency-related income and capital gains. Evading taxes using Bitcoin or any other means is illegal and subject to penalties.

While Bitcoin's price can be volatile, it is essential to distinguish between short-term price fluctuations and its long-term potential as a store of value and global currency. As adoption grows and market liquidity increases, Bitcoin's volatility may stabilize, making it more suitable for everyday transactions.

While speculative trading has been a significant driver of Bitcoin's early adoption, its use cases have expanded over time. From remittances and cross-border transactions to philanthropic donations and micropayments, Bitcoin's versatility extends beyond speculation.

Critics often raise concerns about Bitcoin's energy consumption, citing the energy-intensive mining process. However, it is essential to put Bitcoin's energy use in perspective. Many traditional financial systems consume substantial energy, including banks and data centers. Moreover, the push for renewable energy solutions and the development of energy-efficient consensus mechanisms offer potential solutions to undertake the environmental impact of Bitcoin.

The notion that Bitcoin will entirely replace fiat currencies is a common misconception. While Bitcoin offers an alternative and complementary form of money, the existing financial system is deeply entrenched and unlikely to be entirely displaced in the foreseeable future. Coexistence and integration with traditional financial systems are more plausible scenarios.

Accusations of Bitcoin being a Ponzi scheme have been raised due to its reliance on new investors to sustain its value. However, unlike a Ponzi scheme, Bitcoin operates on a transparent, decentralized blockchain, and its value is not reliant on continuous recruitment. Instead, its value is driven by supply and demand dynamics and the utility it provides to users.

Addressing misconceptions and debunking myths surrounding Bitcoin is essential in fostering a more informed and objective understanding of this revolutionary cryptocurrency. While Bitcoin faces challenges and criticism, separating fact from fiction allows us to recognize its potential as a transformative force in the financial world. By demystifying these misconceptions, we can have more constructive discussions about the opportunities, risks, and implications of Bitcoin's widespread adoption. As the cryptocurrency ecosystem evolves, a nuanced and accurate understanding of Bitcoin will be instrumental in shaping its future impact on global finance and technology.

CHAPTER XIII

The Future of Bitcoin and Cryptocurrencies

Technological developments and upgrades

As the pioneering cryptocurrency, Bitcoin has continuously evolved since its inception in 2009. Over the years, various technological developments and upgrades have been implemented to address scalability, security, and functionality challenges. This section explores the significant technological advancements that have shaped the Bitcoin network, enhancing its performance, security, and user experience.

Introduced in 2017, Segregated Witness (SegWit) was a significant upgrade to resolve the long-standing issue of transaction malleability. This upgrade restructured the way transaction data is stored in blocks, segregating the witness (signature) data from the transaction data. As a result, more transactions can fit within a block, increasing the overall transaction capacity of the Bitcoin network. SegWit also enabled the implementation of second-layer solutions like the Lightning Network, enhancing the scalability and efficiency of Bitcoin's transactions.

The Lightning Network, introduced in 2018, is a second-layer protocol established on top of the Bitcoin blockchain. It addresses the scalability challenge by enabling instantaneous, low-cost microtransactions. By creating off-chain payment channels, users can transact directly with each other without the need for every transaction to be recorded on the blockchain. The Lightning Network significantly reduces transaction fees and processing times, making Bitcoin more practical for everyday transactions and micro-payments.

Schnorr Signatures, a cryptographic improvement, were activated on the Bitcoin network in 2020 through a soft fork. This upgrade replaced the traditional ECDSA (Elliptic Curve Digital Signature Algorithm) signatures with Schnorr Signatures. By aggregating signatures in multi-signature transactions, Schnorr Signatures improve the efficiency of multi-signature transactions, reducing their size and further enhancing scalability. Additionally, Schnorr Signatures offer enhanced privacy by making distinguishing multi-signature transactions from single-signature ones harder.

Scheduled for activation in November 2021 through a soft fork, Taproot is another significant upgrade aimed at enhancing Bitcoin's privacy and functionality. Taproot introduces a new scripting language called Tapscript, which allows for more complex and private smart contract capabilities. This upgrade optimizes the use of Bitcoin's script language, making it more efficient and enabling additional features like cross-chain atomic swaps and more advanced multi-signature schemes.

Activating Schnorr Signatures and Taproot brings several benefits to the Bitcoin network. These upgrades enhance privacy, reduce transaction fees, and improve scalability. Additionally, they open up new possibilities for developing more complex and efficient smart contracts, further expanding Bitcoin's functionality and use cases.
As the demand for Bitcoin grows and the technology surrounding cryptocurrencies continues to advance, more

innovations and upgrades are likely to be proposed and implemented. Improvements in consensus mechanisms, privacy enhancements, and scalability solutions are ongoing research and development areas.

Beyond the Lightning Network, other Layer 2 solutions are being explored to address scalability and transaction throughput. Sidechains like the Liquid Network allow for faster and more confidential transactions by moving them off the main Bitcoin blockchain. These Layer 2 solutions enable many applications, including token issuance, asset transfers, and improved privacy features.

Further research is ongoing to explore the potential implementation of Schnorr Multi-Signatures. This upgrade would combine the benefits of Schnorr Signatures with multi-signature transactions, offering even more significant efficiency gains and further reducing the blockchain's size.

Anticipating the potential threat from quantum computers, research is being conducted to develop quantum-resistant cryptographic algorithms. These algorithms would safeguard Bitcoin against the computational power of future quantum computers, ensuring the long-term security of the network.

In recent years, discussions have emerged around the concept of decentralized governance for Bitcoin protocol upgrades. Proposals like BIP (Bitcoin Improvement Proposal) 8 and BIP 9 aim to introduce a more structured and decentralized approach to protocol upgrades, allowing stakeholders to signal their support or opposition to proposed changes.

Potential challenges and solutions for the future

As the pioneering cryptocurrency, Bitcoin has achieved significant milestones since its inception in 2009. However, as it continues to gain mainstream attention and adoption, several potential challenges lie ahead. In this section, we explore some of the key challenges that Bitcoin might face in the future and discuss possible solutions to ensure its continued growth and success as a global digital currency.

One of the primary challenges for Bitcoin's future is scalability. As the network grows, the demand for transactions increases, leading to congestion and higher transaction fees. The block size limit and the time it takes to process a block pose limitations on the amount of transactions the network can manage per second. Solutions like Segregated Witness (SegWit) and the Lightning Network have already made significant strides in enhancing scalability, but ongoing research and development are necessary to explore additional solutions that can further increase transaction throughput without compromising security.

Bitcoin's energy consumption has drawn both criticism and concern. The energy-intensive proof-of-work mining process requires significant computational power, leading to a substantial carbon footprint. As the call for environmental sustainability grows louder, finding ways to reduce Bitcoin's energy consumption or transitioning to more energy-efficient consensus mechanisms becomes imperative. Exploring alternative consensus mechanisms like proof-of-stake (PoS) or hybrid approaches may provide more sustainable alternatives for the network's long-term viability.

The increasing adoption of Bitcoin has attracted the attention of governments and regulatory authorities worldwide. The decentralized and borderless nature of Bitcoin challenges traditional regulatory frameworks. Balancing fostering innovation and protecting consumers and investors remains a delicate task for policymakers. Collaborative efforts between the cryptocurrency community, industry stakeholders, and regulators are essential to develop clear and adaptive regulatory frameworks that address risks without stifling innovation.

Bitcoin's pseudonymous nature allows for a degree of privacy, but the transparency of the public blockchain can lead to concerns over privacy breaches. Striking a balance between privacy and transparency is crucial, as individuals and businesses require some privacy in their financial transactions. Innovations like Taproot have sought to enhance privacy, but ongoing research and development are necessary to ensure robust and privacy-preserving solutions.

Ensuring interoperability between different blockchain networks is vital in a rapidly evolving cryptocurrency ecosystem. Bitcoin's compatibility with other cryptocurrencies and blockchain platforms enables seamless and efficient cross-chain transactions. Developments like atomic swaps and interoperability protocols aim to bridge the gap between disparate blockchain networks, creating a more interconnected and efficient financial system.

As mining becomes increasingly competitive and resource-intensive, concerns over mining centralization arise. Large mining pools with significant hashing power can potentially control the network's consensus, raising centralization risks. Continued efforts to encourage decentralization through community engagement, mining pool diversification, and promoting smaller-scale mining operations are essential to mitigate centralization risks.

For Bitcoin to achieve mainstream adoption, user experience must be improved. Acquiring, storing, and using Bitcoin should be user-friendly and accessible to individuals with varying technical expertise. Enhanced wallet security, seamless payment solutions, and educational resources can contribute to a more user-friendly ecosystem, encouraging broader adoption.

Bitcoin's prominence and the value it holds make it an attractive target for malicious actors. Cybersecurity threats, such as hacking attempts, phishing attacks, and potential vulnerabilities in the network's code, pose risks to users and the overall stability of the network. Vigilance in identifying and mitigating security threats and ongoing audits and code reviews are vital to maintaining the network's integrity and security.

As Bitcoin's adoption grows, ensuring financial inclusion for all individuals becomes crucial. Access to financial services and digital assets should not be limited to those with access to modern banking systems. Efforts to improve financial literacy, promote accessibility to cryptocurrencies, and support communities in developing countries can foster greater financial inclusion and empowerment.

Bitcoin's decentralized nature means that decision-making relies on achieving consensus among the community. Engaging in open dialogue, addressing differing viewpoints, and seeking consensus on crucial upgrades and improvements are vital to maintaining Bitcoin's integrity and avoiding contentious hard forks.

Bitcoin's role in the evolving financial landscape

Since its launch in 2009, Bitcoin—the first decentralized cryptocurrency in history—has caused significant disruptions in the financial sector. As a peer-to-peer digital currency, Bitcoin operates without intermediaries like banks, challenging traditional financial systems and reshaping how we perceive and utilize money. In this section, we delve into Bitcoin's role in the evolving financial landscape, examining its impact on various aspects of finance and its potential implications for the future.

One of the most significant contributions of Bitcoin to the financial landscape is its potential to enhance financial inclusion. In regions with insufficient access to traditional banking services, Bitcoin provides an alternative means for individuals to participate in the global economy. With only an internet connection, anyone can create a Bitcoin wallet and transact with others, regardless of their location or background. By empowering the unbanked and underbanked populations, Bitcoin opens doors to new economic opportunities and fosters greater financial independence.

Bitcoin's decentralized nature, enabled by its underlying blockchain technology, introduces a paradigm shift in how trust is established within the financial system. Instead of relying on central authorities, such as banks or governments, to validate and record transactions, Bitcoin utilizes a distributed network of nodes to achieve consensus. This decentralization eliminates the requirement for intermediaries, reducing transaction costs and enhancing the security and transparency of financial transactions.

Traditional financial systems often face limitations when conducting cross-border transactions. International transfers can be slow, expensive, and subject to various regulatory hurdles. Bitcoin transcends these limitations by allowing borderless transactions in a matter of minutes, regardless of the transaction amount. Its global reach and peer-to-peer nature make it a preferred option for individuals and businesses seeking a fast and cost-effective way to move funds across borders.

Bitcoin's scarcity and fixed supply of 21 million coins make it an attractive store of value, particularly in times of economic uncertainty. As a non-inflationary digital asset, Bitcoin offers an alternative to traditional fiat currencies that may be subject to inflationary pressures. Many investors view Bitcoin as a potential hedge against inflation and store of value asset, similar to gold, which has further solidified its position in the financial landscape.

Beyond its use as a medium of exchange, Bitcoin has evolved into a sought-after investment asset class. While sometimes considered a challenge, its price volatility has also attracted investors seeking high returns. Institutional interest in Bitcoin has grown, with prominent companies and asset management firms adding Bitcoin to their investment portfolios. As its adoption as an investment asset increases, Bitcoin's influence on financial markets and traditional investment strategies becomes more pronounced.

The emergence of Bitcoin has catalyzed a wave of innovation in the broader financial technology (FinTech) industry. Blockchain technology, the foundation of Bitcoin, has been adopted and adapted for various use cases beyond cryptocurrencies. From smart contracts to decentralized finance (DeFi) applications, the underlying principles of Bitcoin have inspired a wide range of technological advancements that could revolutionize financial services in the future.

Bitcoin's disruptive nature has also presented regulatory challenges for governments and financial authorities worldwide. As it operates outside the traditional banking system, its decentralized and pseudonymous nature can be perceived as a potential facilitator of illicit activities. Striking a balance between embracing innovation and safeguarding against misuse has prompted policymakers to explore appropriate regulatory frameworks to address consumer protection, financial stability, and anti-money laundering (AML) concerns without stifling innovation.

As Bitcoin's adoption grows, ensuring financial inclusion for all individuals becomes crucial. Access to financial services and digital assets should not be limited to those with access to modern banking systems. Efforts to improve financial literacy, promote accessibility to cryptocurrencies, and support communities in developing countries can foster greater financial inclusion and empowerment.

Bitcoin's decentralized nature means that decision-making relies on achieving consensus among the community. Engaging in open dialogue, addressing differing viewpoints, and seeking consensus on crucial upgrades and improvements are vital to maintaining Bitcoin's integrity and avoiding contentious hard forks.

Despite its remarkable impact on the financial landscape, Bitcoin faces challenges that must be addressed for sustained growth and broader adoption. Scalability, energy consumption, regulatory uncertainties, and user experience are among the key hurdles that must be tackled. Technological advancements, research, and collaboration within the cryptocurrency community and with regulators will play vital roles in overcoming these challenges.

The future of Bitcoin in the evolving financial landscape is promising. As adoption increases, its influence on global financial systems is likely to grow exponentially. Further development of Layer 2 solutions, regulatory clarity, enhanced user experience, and broader education about Bitcoin's benefits are expected to pave the way for its continued integration into mainstream financial services.

CONCLUSION

Recap of key points covered

In this comprehensive book, we have journeyed through the fascinating world of Bitcoin, the pioneering cryptocurrency that has revolutionized the financial landscape. From its creation to its potential future impact, each chapter has explored crucial aspects of Bitcoin, shedding light on its significance in shaping the global economy and financial systems. As we conclude this book, let us recapitulate the key points covered in each section to provide a holistic understanding of Bitcoin's journey and its transformative potential.

The book began with exploring Bitcoin's creation and its enigmatic creator, Satoshi Nakamoto. We discussed the groundbreaking Bitcoin whitepaper and how it introduced the concept of a peer-to-peer digital currency that operates without intermediaries. The overall supply of 21 million coins and the underlying blockchain technology's decentralized nature were emphasized as essential elements that set Bitcoin apart from traditional fiat currencies.

Next, we delved into the technological principles behind Bitcoin's security. We discussed the role of cryptographic techniques, such as public and private keys, in securing transactions and controlling users' digital assets. The mining process and consensus mechanisms like Proof of Work (or PoW) and Proof of Stake (or PoS) were elucidated for their critical roles in ensuring the network's integrity and preventing double-spending.

Environmental concerns and energy consumption were subjects of the subsequent section. We examined the debate surrounding Bitcoin's environmental impact and explored potential solutions to make its energy usage more sustainable. Balancing the need for network security with environmental responsibility emerged as a challenge that the cryptocurrency community continues to address.

The book unraveled the intricacies of Bitcoin transactions, from their structure to the importance of transaction fees and confirmations. We highlighted the significance of nodes in validating transactions and maintaining the decentralized nature of the Bitcoin network.

Comparisons to traditional fiat currencies were the focus of the subsequent section. We emphasized Bitcoin's advantages in borderless transactions, financial inclusion, and its potential as a store of value and investment asset. Furthermore, we debunked misconceptions surrounding Bitcoin to provide a clearer understanding of its true potential and limitations.

Bitcoin's role in cross-border remittances and its potential to reduce transaction fees were discussed in the subsequent chapters. We explored case studies of Bitcoin adoption in developing countries, underscoring how it has empowered individuals and communities with insufficient access to traditional financial services.

The impact of Bitcoin on the evolving financial landscape was extensively examined, emphasizing its contributions to financial inclusion, decentralization, and fostering innovation. We addressed Bitcoin's regulatory challenges and the potential implications of its widespread adoption on the global financial stage.

Challenges and potential solutions for Bitcoin's future were discussed in detail. Scalability, energy consumption, regulatory uncertainty, and user experience were identified as key hurdles that require collective efforts and technological advancements to overcome.

The final section of the book offered a reflection on the broader significance of Bitcoin's impact. We examined how Bitcoin's influence extends beyond being merely a digital currency, sparking debates on the future of money, the role of central banks, and the quest for financial autonomy and sovereignty. The growth of blockchain technology and the potential for decentralized finance (DeFi) were also acknowledged as transformative consequences of Bitcoin's existence.

In conclusion, this book has taken readers on an informative and thought-provoking journey through the realms of Bitcoin. From its mysterious inception to its potential to reshape the global financial landscape, Bitcoin has captured the world's imagination and challenged conventional notions of money and value exchange. Its significance reaches far beyond its monetary value, symbolizing a shift towards a more decentralized, inclusive, and innovative financial future.

As we move forward, the lessons learned from Bitcoin's past and the insights gained from its present will undoubtedly shape the trajectory of this groundbreaking technology. Collaborative efforts, regulatory clarity, and ongoing technological advancements will play a pivotal role in unlocking Bitcoin's full potential and ensuring a prosperous and equitable future for the world of finance. Bitcoin's journey is far from over, and its impact on the world of finance is poised to endure for generations to come.

Final thoughts on the significance of Bitcoin's impact

Throughout this extensive exploration of Bitcoin's journey, technological principles, financial implications, and potential future prospects, it becomes evident that Bitcoin's impact on the world goes beyond being just a digital currency. Bitcoin's significance transcends its monetary value; it symbolizes a paradigm shift in how we perceive and engage with money and financial systems. In this final reflection, we delve into the overarching significance of Bitcoin's impact, touching upon its contributions, challenges, and the broader implications it holds for the future of finance.

At its core, Bitcoin represents a revolution in the concept of money and value exchange. Providing a decentralized, peer-to-peer, and transparent system challenges traditional financial intermediaries, like banks and governments, and empowers individuals with financial autonomy. Creating a fixed supply of 21 million coins and using cryptographic principles to secure transactions have instilled trust in Bitcoin as a store of value and investment asset, attracting both retail and institutional investors seeking an alternative to fiat currencies.

Bitcoin's impact extends far beyond its role as a digital currency. The underlying blockchain technology has sparked a wave of innovation, propelling the development of countless cryptocurrencies and decentralized applications. This has given rise to the broader concept of decentralized finance (DeFi), where traditional financial services are being reinvented with decentralized and trustless systems, reducing reliance on intermediaries and enhancing financial accessibility for all.

Financial inclusion stands as one of the most profound contributions of Bitcoin to the world. It has granted millions of unbanked and underbanked individuals worldwide access to financial services and digital assets. Bitcoin's borderless nature allows for instant and low-cost transactions, breaking down barriers that previously hindered cross-border financial interactions. For those living in regions with volatile economies and limited access to stable financial systems, Bitcoin has emerged as a beacon of hope and a means of preserving wealth.

However, despite its remarkable contributions, Bitcoin faces challenges that require careful consideration and strategic solutions. Scalability remains a persistent concern as the network seeks to handle increasing transaction volumes without compromising security. Energy consumption and environmental concerns have prompted calls for more energy-efficient consensus mechanisms and sustainable mining practices. Balancing regulatory compliance and fostering innovation is critical to avoid stifling the growth of this disruptive technology.

The significance of Bitcoin's impact on the financial landscape goes beyond its immediate role as a digital currency. It has spurred a global conversation about the future of money, the role of central banks, and the need for financial democratization. Governments and central banks have taken notice of the potential of digital currencies and are exploring the development of CBDCs, also known as central bank digital currencies, to enhance financial systems and maintain control over monetary policies.

Bitcoin's journey is symbolic of humanity's ongoing quest for financial autonomy, privacy, and sovereignty. It has sparked debates about the nature of money, the implications of decentralized systems, and the balance between personal freedoms and regulatory oversight. As Bitcoin continues to evolve and influence the financial world, it is a testament to the power of collective collaboration, technological innovation, and the resilience of an idea that challenges the status quo.

The impact of Bitcoin extends not only to individuals and businesses but also to nations. Some countries have embraced Bitcoin as a viable payment option, while others have expressed concerns about its potential effect on financial stability and the risks of money laundering and terrorism financing. As more countries grapple with the implications of digital currencies, international cooperation and dialogue will be crucial to finding a balanced approach to regulation that fosters innovation while addressing legitimate concerns.

As we conclude this exploration of Bitcoin's significance, it is essential to recognize that its journey is far from over. The future of Bitcoin remains both promising and uncertain, filled with potential advancements, regulatory developments, and challenges that will shape its trajectory. The lessons learned from Bitcoin's past provide valuable insights into how digital currencies can foster financial inclusion, redefine trust, and reimagine financial systems in ways previously thought impossible.

In the grand tapestry of human history, Bitcoin is a testament to the power of an idea that sparked a revolution. Its impact on the financial sector will continue to unfold and reverberate through generations, transforming how we understand and engage with money. As we look to the future, we must embrace the innovative spirit that has driven Bitcoin's success, foster collaboration, and collectively work toward a more inclusive, transparent, and equitable financial landscape—one where the principles of decentralization and trust offer hope for a better and more resilient financial future.

Thank you for buying and reading/ listening to our book. If you found this book useful/ helpful please take a few minutes and leave a review on the platform where you purchased our book. Your feedback matters greatly to us.